Budgeting and Negotiating Fees with Clients: A Lawyer's Guide

SALLY DYSON

Globe Law
and Business

Author
Sally Dyson

Published by
Globe Law and Business Ltd
3 Mylor Close
Horsell
Woking
Surrey GU21 4DD
United Kingdom
Tel: +44 20 3745 4770
www.globelawandbusiness.com

ISBN: 978-1-90778-793-5
A catalogue record for this book is available from the British Library

Contents

Executive summary

WITH LEGAL fees coming under increasing scrutiny, all law firms, whether they charge by the hour or operate alternative fee arrangements (AFAs) will need to negotiate fees; be it a discount to an hourly rate or a year-long fixed retainer. Budgeting and negotiating skills will be needed by all fee earners with responsibility for agreeing any fees or discounts. The more a firm uses AFAs, the more important budgeting and negotiating becomes.

Most legal training focuses on black letter law and technical legal skills. Fee earners may be unprepared to deal with client demands on fees. The systems, processes and management information in law firms are generally predicated on the assumption of standard hourly charge-out rates. Fee earners often lack the information and tools that they need to make accurate matter cost predictions, and the ability or incentive to manage matters cost effectively. Without this information, their negotiating positions are also undermined. This report will help both individual lawyers and firm leaders to plug the skills gap by analysing the problems faced. It provides novel approaches, step-by-step guides and practical tools for improving individual behaviour and firm-wide processes, and inspires readers to make changes by following the example of others. As the case studies cited in this report confirm, the rewards for firms which achieve best practice in budgeting and negotiating include increased profits, strengthened client relationships and competitive advantage.

A key tenet of this report is that negotiation does not have to be about winners and losers. A successful negotiation can be one in which both parties feel that they have secured a commercial result which meets their objectives. By concluding mutually satisfying negotiations, law firms will generate profitable, strong and long-term client relationships, thereby securing their future financial health and fostering successful individual careers.

Chapter 1 of this report describes the various approaches to fees taken by law firms and coins the phrase 'universal law firm fee continuum' or 'continuum'. Readers will recognise their firms in the descriptions and find their places on the continuum. Establishing a firm's position on the continuum will highlight the aspects of the report which will be most relevant for each reader. Some readers may be contemplating making greater use of AFAs, but are wary of the consequences and unsure if AFAs can be managed profitably.

Chapter 2 examines the rise of AFAs and explains why they are intensifying the need for lawyers to hone their budgeting and negotiating skills.

The report continues, in Chapter 3, to address the reasons that many lawyers are sceptical or fearful of AFAs. It also shows how firms can counter the perceived downsides of AFAs through better budgeting and negotiating.

Having established the need for well-honed budgeting and negotiating skills, Chapter 4 goes on to set out the key financial measures that all lawyers need to understand. This chapter de-mystifies some critical financial concepts and explains their relevance for preparing budgets and negotiating fees with clients.

Chapter 5 continues to take the reader through the elements needed to understand the cost, to the law firm, of conducting a matter. It then builds on this information to show how to create a matter budget.

Chapter 6 tackles the all-important question of how to stick to a budget and incorporates an overview of legal project management, written for this report by Pamela Woldow and Douglas Richardson of Edge International.

Chapter 7 turns to negotiation, starting with how to overcome the common obstacles to effective fee negotiation that are faced by lawyers.

Chapter 8 explains how to take control of the negotiation process from preparation through to closing, and Chapter 9 focuses on how to ask for (and get) the desired fees and structures; primarily by demonstrating value to the client.

Chapter 10 follows with a wealth of tips, tactics and tricks, covering everything from how to act, through opening gambits and walk-away points, to traps to avoid.

The report goes much further. Knowing what needs to be done is only part of the battle. Gaining acceptance of new techniques and ways of working across the firm is much harder. Chapter 11 guides firm leaders seeking to develop and communicate a strategy for better budgeting and negotiating, while Chapter 12 deals with implementing and embedding best practice across the firm. These chapters will be particularly useful for anyone charged with turning a firm's strategy into reality – whether that strategy is to increase profitability through deployment of AFAs, or simply to increase realisation through better negotiation. The vital importance of communication, empowering employees, optimising support services and aligning incentives is shown. These chapters provide valuable insights for firm leaders, be they the managing partner, practice area head or leader of a support service function.

There are detailed case studies at the end of this report, all based on personal and up-to-date interviews. Case study 1 features an interview with Tim Aspinall, managing partner at UK top-100 firm DMH Stallard. He describes the award-winning business tools introduced by the firm for budgeting, negotiating and communicating with clients – and the impact that they have had on the firm's business.

Case study 2 relates to Crowell & Moring, an AmLaw 100 firm, which successfully operates value-based billing.

Case study 3 presents a client perspective, from a legal procurement manager, who sheds light on the methods that are commonly used by procurement professionals and provides observations on law firm negotiating technique.

This report concludes with three practical tools to enable readers to start putting the lessons learnt throughout the commentary into immediate practice. Appendix 1 contains a matter plan template, which is an essential component of a matter budget. A matter budget template itself is set out at Appendix 2. Appendix 3 comprises a pre-negotiation checklist, which reminds lawyers of the information that they need in order to negotiate effectively and organises that information very concisely.

Readers of this report will develop an appreciation of how their approaches to budgeting and negotiation impact the prosperity and sustainability of their firms and why astute budgeting and negotiation is more important than ever. They will be guided in how to adopt best practices in budgeting and negotiation, both for themselves as individuals and across their firms. The advice in this report is supported by case studies which demonstrate the tried and tested nature of the methodologies advocated and by practical tools which can be adapted to suit readers' own practices.

About the author

SALLY DYSON is the director of Firm Sense Limited, a specialist consultancy providing client relationship evaluation and advice exclusively to law firms. Sally qualified as a solicitor and practised at Slaughter and May. She then worked as an in-house lawyer for nearly a decade before moving on from the practice of law to found Firm Sense.

Sally combines expertise in client listening with an in-depth understanding of law firms and their clients. Sally advises law firms on aligning organisational practices and individual behaviour with client needs in order to improve client retention, win business and improve cash flow and profitability.

Sally Dyson can be contacted by email at: sallydyson@firmsense.co.uk. For more information about Sally or Firm Sense please visit: http://www.firmsense.co.uk

Acknowledgements

I WRITE in Chapter 12, citing Jo Owen, that leadership is a team sport and the same could be said of the writing of this report. Far from being a mere desk-top exercise, I have been lucky enough to receive advice, information and contributions, freely given, from a wide range of lawyers and consultants. Special mentions must go to:

- Tim Aspinall of DMH Stallard and Robert Lipstein and Joel Wheeler of Crowell & Moring, who participated in the case studies at the end of this report;
- Robert Mowbray of Taylor Mowbray, who first introduced me to the matter budget and generously donated his materials;
- Pamela Woldow and Douglas Richardson of Edge International, whose very topical piece on legal project management can be found in Chapter 6;
- Laura Watkins and Shani Ospina of The Cognitas Group, and their colleague Jo Owen, who inducted me in the mysteries of change management and kindly provided materials for this report. They also introduced me to Kara Stenhouse, who converted my pencil scribbles into the figures and appendices laid out here;
- Toby Brown of 3 Geeks and a Law Blog fame, for his thoughts on aligning support services with pricing strategy; and
- Stephanie Ramasamy who, to my surprise, invited me to write this report.

There are many other unsung contributors who have provided suggestions, anecdotes and introductions but who prefer to remain anonymous. They know who they are and I thank them.

I have spent many pleasant hours soaking up information in the delightful surroundings of both the British Library and the Law Society Library. Of the books that I read in those august institutions, I have particularly relied on:

- *The End of Lawyers?* By Richard Susskind;
- Ronald Baker's *Implementing Value Pricing;*
- Roger Fisher and William Ury's *Getting to Yes,* as well as Nic Peeling's *Brilliant Negotiations;*
- Kim Cameron and Robert Quinn on *Diagnosing and Changing Organizational Culture;* and
- John Kotter's *Leading Change.*

Numerous other thought leaders and experts are referenced in the text.

All has been made possible by the support, interest and tolerance of family and friends, who have encouraged me whilst this report has been in gestation. Most particularly, my husband, parents and children – the latter are still wondering what on earth can be in this report that it has taken so long to write.

PART ONE

Understanding law firm fee models, budgeting and negotiation

Chapter 1: The universal law firm fee continuum

"The pricing structures being used by firms and clients to pay for legal services are diversifying, but there is not yet always a clear understanding of how to use pricing to reflect the economic value of the work delivered and how to use it to bring firms' and clients' objectives into closer alignment." Winmark

LAW FIRMS come in many shapes and sizes. Some have thousands of lawyers and span many continents, such as DLA Piper, with 4,200 fee earners spread over 30 offices. At the opposite end of the spectrum there are sole principals trading on the high street.

Size is not the only differentiating factor. In an ever more globalized and litigious society, where regulation is increasing exponentially, the breadth of legal practice areas and the list of legal specialisms continues to expand. Islamic finance, emissions trading and digital rights management are three such flourishing, progressive fields in the disparate practice areas of finance, environmental protection and media law, which were relatively unknown only a decade ago.

Whichever fields a law firm chooses to specialise in and whatever the size and scale of its practice, all law firms must grapple with the fundamental questions of how much to charge their clients and how to get paid.

Fee models adopted by law firms

The fees that can be commanded by a single practitioner acting in a divorce will be leagues apart from those which a White Shoe firm in New York or a Magic Circle firm in London can expect to earn on the securitisation of a billion dollar property portfolio. Yet throughout the second half of the 20th century, both types of firm would have expected to charge their clients on the basis of set hourly rates. The rates and the number of hours worked would have varied but the charging methodology would have been the same.

However, in the face of mounting agitation from clients in recent years, many law firms have been forced, or have chosen, to reconsider this charging model. As a result, firms are increasingly offering their clients a variety of alternative fee arrangements (AFAs) for at least some types of work. Types of AFA now available in the market place include: fixed fees, caps, collars, contingency fees and value billing. The mechanics of these fee types and more are all explained in Case Study 2, which examines how one US firm (Crowell & Moring) successfully operates AFAs.

This report does not attempt to provide a comprehensive overview of the wealth of publications and press comment on the pros and cons of hourly rates.[1] However, Chapter 2 examines the rise of AFAs and the extent to which they are intensifying the need for lawyers to possess budgeting and negotiating skills.

Chapter 3 acknowledges the perceived risks of AFAs to law firms, and how these risks can be mitigated and turned to reward, through effective use of budgeting and negotiating skills.

Introducing the universal law firm fee continuum

Just as law firms' size, shape and strengths are diverse, so are their approaches to fees. As Winmark, a research consultancy which also runs professional networks, has observed, "the pricing structures being used by firms and clients to pay for legal services are diversifying, but there is not yet always a clear understanding of how to use pricing to reflect the economic value of the work delivered and how to use it to bring firms' and clients' objectives into closer alignment."[2] This report will help practitioners to do just that.

At one end of the scale, there are numbers of firms which resolutely insist on charging only on the basis of hourly rates. At the other end of the scale there are firms, such as Valorem Law, which no longer charge on the basis of hourly rates at all. Many firms are at a point in between the two extremes of the spectrum, but all firms will feature somewhere on it. For the purposes of this report, the spectrum is referred to as the 'universal law firm fee continuum' or 'continuum' for short. The continuum is shown in Figure 1 and will be referred to throughout the remainder of this chapter, which examines in more detail:

- The various positions that law firms currently hold on the continuum (by accident or design);
- What this means in terms of their fee behaviour;
- How this behaviour affects the financial health and success of the firm; and
- The circumstances in which each type of firm will need to call on budgeting and negotiating skills.

Common positions on the continuum

The continuum extends from firms on the left of the scale, which operate solely on the basis of after-the-event, hourly-rate-based billing to those on the right, which always prepare matter budgets in advance of commencing new matters and negotiate fees with their clients before starting any work. Firms could find themselves at any point on the continuum but for the purposes of this report, four positions have been selected at the points labelled A to D. A one-word description of the approach to budgeting and negotiating fees exhibited at each of the marked positions is set out in the list below:

- **A**voiding;
- **B**egrudging;
- **C**onflicting; and
- **D**elivering.

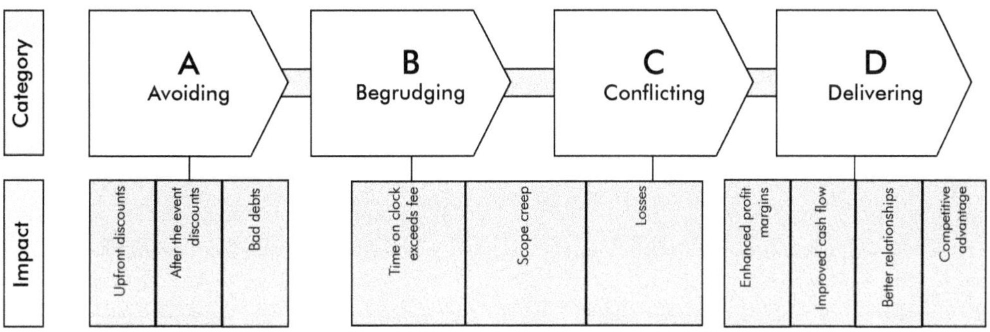

Figure 1: The universal law firm fee continuum

The paragraphs which follow analyse the behaviour of firms at each of the marked positions on the continuum in more detail, in order to illustrate how – and why – despite their divergent approaches to fees, lawyers at such firms will all find themselves in need of budgeting and negotiating skills.

Avoiding

Firms at position A on the continuum are those which rely exclusively on hourly rates and studiously avoid offering their clients any AFAs. In the current economic climate and in light of increasing client sophistication and activism, they will find themselves besieged by clients pressing for discounts. Requests for discounted hourly rates may occur as the relationship is being set up or during a panel review. Many law firms will agree ten to 15 per cent discounts to standard hourly rates for all matters undertaken for specific clients.

Alternatively, discounts may be requested by clients at the end of matters. Such discounts may be asked for before invoices have been rendered, or they may be insisted upon after invoices have been delivered but remain unpaid by clients who find the quantum unacceptable. Again, it is not uncommon for clients to ask for ten to 15 per cent. Law firms are increasingly finding that even those clients that benefit from pre-agreed discounted rates also demand additional discounts at the end of matters. This can add up to a hefty 20 to 30 per cent total discount (not including additional hours that get written off by partners before invoices are issued, or by assistants who under-record their time). Such discounts may wipe out the firm's entire profit on some matters.

Firms which bill only on the basis of hourly rates are also often pressurised, by their clients, to provide fee estimates even though they are not set up to do so. However much a firm emphasises that the estimate is non-binding, once a client has an estimate in mind, they will be disappointed if the estimate is exceeded. Firms at position A on the continuum are rarely well prepared to provide estimates because their systems are all designed to facilitate cost plus billing and not for producing or managing matter budgets.

Lawyers in these firms may have traditionally assumed that they did not need to get to grips with budgeting and negotiating fees as their rates were set by the managing partner, finance director, or a group of senior members of the firm. However, now that they are being assailed on all sides with demands for discounts, it is critical that fee earners understand the cost to the firm of the work that they are performing. They must know the profit margins that they are required to deliver and develop skills which enable them to achieve the fees that their financial model requires.

Begrudging

Firms at position B on the continuum will succumb to pressure from important clients and begrudgingly offer AFAs on an *ad hoc* basis. Each time an AFA is agreed, it is treated as an exception to the general principle that the firm bills on the basis of hourly rates. Each attempt at an AFA confirms the suspicions of firms at position B that AFAs cannot be managed profitably and should be resisted whenever possible.

Firms at position B look forward to the day when the boom times will return and lawyers can move on from the unhelpful focus on fees and get on with the business of lawyering. In the meantime, firms at position B have not invested in systems or processes which would enable their lawyers to predict likely matter cost accurately, or to draw up matter plans and budgets. Nor have their lawyers been provided with training in budgeting and negotiating as the need for these skills is not recognised. It is unlikely that such firms indulge in any of the more exotic AFAs offered by their competitors, such as holdbacks and value fees, but they are more than likely to have to concede fixed or capped fees for at least some of their work. Inevitably they will find that their time on the clock regularly exceeds the amount of the fixed or capped fee that was quoted. This can lead to painful discussions with their clients where they explain that they did more work than they had intended. They may find that their attempts to recoup their time costs are rebuffed by their clients (and few firms want to sue their clients for fees). Such firms will only be able to swallow the financial hit from AFAs that have gone wrong if the majority of their work is billed on the basis of hourly rates.

Firms at position B, like those at position A, have their heads buried in the sand when it comes to budgeting and negotiating, but the need for them to develop budgeting and negotiating skills becomes all the more acute as they find themselves called upon to work on the basis of AFAs by an increasing proportion of their clients and across greater numbers of matter types.

Conflicting

Leaders of firms at position C have decided that their firms need to change if they are to survive and prosper in the modern legal market place. Managing partners, finance directors, heads of business development, knowledge management (KM) and IT may have all agreed that their firm's fee earners need to get better at budgeting and negotiating fees with clients. They may have invested heavily in creating management information and budgeting tools for their fee earners. They will have provided training sessions for their partners and perhaps some assistants, in how to use the tools and how to discuss fees with clients. They may have issued policies on when AFAs can be used and they may have announced that use of the budgeting tools is now mandatory.

Strangely, their proclamations may have fallen on deaf ears. Their fee earners still show a marked preference for billing on the basis of hourly rates. When they do offer AFAs, they are very often loss-making. The expensively produced budgeting tools are rarely used. Chapters 11 and 12 analyse the reasons why law firms may find themselves in the position where their stated strategy and the behaviour of their fee earners conflicts. Despite their intention to embrace the new world order they find themselves suffering from the same problems as the firms at position B on the continuum. They may even be worse off as they have sunk costs into training and tools.

Firms at position C have already recognised (at the leadership level at least) the need for budgeting and negotiating skills. Their aim now must be to persuade the rest of the firm of this wisdom and to ensure that best-practice budgeting and negotiating is embedded within the firm.

Delivering

Firms at position D are the closest to billing nirvana. There will always be scope for further performance improvement but such firms are consistently delivering matters within budget and are successfully negotiating profitable fees with their clients. They may be operating on the basis of hourly rates or AFAs. Either way, such firms will have taught their fee earners to understand law firm finance and will have provided them with budgeting tools which enable them to calculate the likely cost to the firm of any given matter.

Firms at position D will also have trained their fee earners in how to negotiate fees with clients. Not only will the tools and training have been provided but the vast majority of fee earners will have bought into the precepts espoused by the firm's leaders and will be adhering to them.

These firms can take a moment to pat themselves on the back. However, they must not rest on their laurels or they may be overtaken by other firms which are continuing to innovate and improve their budgeting and negotiating behaviour.

Why firms must progress along the continuum

As has been shown, all law firms will sit somewhere on the continuum. They may fall neatly into one of the categories A to D or slot in somewhere in-between. Firms may not be internally consistent. One practice group within the firm may exhibit characteristics of a firm at position A, while another practice group may behave more like a firm at position B. Firms do not necessarily make a straight line progression along the continuum. Indeed, moving from position A to position B may not feel like progress at all, as financial results may get worse rather than better as firms dabble inexpertly in AFAs.

However, regardless of whether they intend to operate AFAs, all firms should aspire to reach position D on the continuum. The benefits accrued by these firms are manifold. All things being equal, such firms can expect to achieve more consistent and sustainable profit margins which are in line with the firm's strategic plans. All the firm's fee earners know the acceptable margin range each matter must produce and what this means in terms of rates or fees that they can charge. They will understand how to plan for matter profitability and how to keep matters on track. They will have learnt how to demonstrate their value to clients so that rates and fees are agreed and paid. Not only are they paid, but they are paid on time.

Cash flow has been an enormous issue for firms in the downturn. Many firms have seen their work reduced and in addition to demanding discounts, clients have been taking longer to pay. There may still be an element of foot dragging by clients' accounts payable departments but when fees have been agreed in advance, clients find it easy to sign-off bills as soon as they are received. Firms charging on an hourly basis will normally have more of an uphill struggle getting their bills paid than those using AFAs, as they need to justify their bills to their clients at the end of each matter when their bargaining power is low. However, firms which have become skilled in recognising where they add value and have mastered negotiating techniques will have a great deal more success than those which have not.

Of equal importance, firms at position D will most likely reap the rewards of better client relationships. The acts of budgeting and negotiating encourage law firms to develop deep understanding of their clients. In fact, to budget and negotiate effectively, the law firm will be expected to enter discussions proactively with its clients about their goals and priorities. Budgets will be more accurate if firms understand how their clients operate – for example, whether they are thrusting and commercial, or follow cumbersome processes. The process of agreeing fees together can bring law firms closer to their clients and this closeness is very much enhanced when the firm delivers invoices which the client considers to be good value. The majority of firms are not yet approaching position D on the continuum. Firms that do get there will benefit from significant competitive advantage.

References

1. The reader is referred to *Alternative Fee Arrangements: Value Fees and the Changing Legal Market*, Patrick Lamb, Ark Conferences Limited, 2010
2. *Winmark Looking Glass Report: The Legal World on its Future*, Winmark, London 2010

Chapter 2: How alternative fee arrangements are intensifying the need for budgeting and negotiating skills

"The old system, one that has allowed lawyers to under-perform and overcharge, is to be replaced by a new model... the free market is coming soon to the world of law."
Richard Susskind

Alternative fees now: Hype or reality

"Magic Circle partner fees have risen by more than 50 per cent in the past five years," trumpeted *The Lawyer* magazine in September 2010.[1] The article went on to reveal that, since 2005, the average headline rate commanded by a partner in one of the UK's magic circle[2] firms had increased from £425 per hour to £650 per hour. Some stellar partners were able to achieve considerably higher rates than that. Reading these figures, it might be tempting to think that such high earners can sit back and relax while the money rolls in. But a quick reality check, even amongst those in the magic circle, will show that most practitioners are feeling the economic pinch. Headline rates may appear positive but realised rates may be much lower as firms are forced to offer discounts to win work, retain clients or get their bills paid.

Commentators have heralded the demise of the hourly rate for years but this method of charging clients has hung on stubbornly despite the well-rehearsed arguments against it. In its 2011 survey, Winmark[3] found that hourly rates were still the most commonly used method for calculating fees, with 79 per cent of the clients surveyed reporting that they frequently used hourly rates. Whilst this proves that hourly rates continue to dominate in the high-end legal market, it should be noted that the previous year's survey had found that 85 per cent of such clients were frequently using hourly rates. Whilst the proportion of clients still making frequent use of hourly rates remains high there has been a significant drop in a short period, which follows the expected trend.

While there is no disputing the continued preponderance of hourly rates in clients' dealings with law firms; use and satisfaction are very different. The *Legal Week* Intelligence *Client Satisfaction Report 2010'*[4] found that hourly billing was the preferred method of only nine per cent of clients, falling further to only three per cent amongst the really big clients (spending over £50m per year on legal fees). Further, *Legal Week* found that client satisfaction with their law firms' approaches to fees and billing had actually fallen in the previous 12 months. *Legal Week* concluded that it was not credible that law firms were making fewer efforts to please their clients. On the contrary, it suggested that clients were becoming more demanding and were calling for ever more sophisticated and flexible approaches to fees.

Having said that, it would not be true or fair to say that all clients want AFAs all of the time.

Some law firms are surprised and disappointed when their attempts to offer AFAs to certain clients are rejected. There are still areas of work, such as complex litigation, large corporate transactions and cutting-edge advisory work where the majority of clients feel that AFAs would be inappropriate and prefer to fall back on hourly rates. Altman Weil[5] found that clients often consider that these areas of work are either too unpredictable or important for fees to be agreed upfront. However, there are many instances of large corporate clients successfully using AFAs even in the most complicated, high value and business-critical matters.

The Association of Corporate Counsel (ACC) website[6] cites numerous examples. The reluctance of some clients to embrace AFAs in such circumstances can therefore be ascribed to:

- Lack of time and resources to structure an AFA at the start of an urgent and important matter;
- Lack of confidence in their own (and the law firm's) ability to accurately scope the work at the outset;
- Lack of confidence in the firm being able to work within an agreed budget; and
- Fear that quality will be sacrificed by the firm in the interests of saving costs.

As firms and clients become more expert at budgeting and negotiating AFAs, they will be used for increasingly complex, high value, and bespoke transactions.

Continued forces of change

Opinion remains divided amongst law firms as to whether AFAs will gain further traction or will quietly disappear when the boom times return. Without doubt, attacks are being mounted on hourly rates from a variety of quarters. The principal threats to hourly rates are summarised briefly below.

Client activism

The main reason that firms have begun offering AFAs is that their clients have insisted upon it. As Winmark highlighted in its 2010 report, "General Counsel crave simplicity, clarity and predictability; while firms need to develop pricing structures that create a clear economic link between how much they cost their clients and the value they create for their clients' businesses."[7]

The ACC has been one of the most vocal and powerful orchestrators of client activism. It launched its Value Challenge in February 2010. The ACC described the impetus for this drive to achieve better value for law firm clients as follows: "For the past two decades, there has been an unrelenting drive by companies and their suppliers to reduce costs while increasing quality and value in their products and services. The only outlier seemed to be the law firms… Here's a stunning fact: according to a recent issue of the California Bar Journal…'while non-law firm costs increased by 20 per cent over the past ten years, large law firms' prices jumped almost 75 per cent in the same period'. These numbers confirm the disconnect most if not all of us have been feeling."

Although the ACC is a membership organisation, most of its materials on the Value Challenge are also available to non-members. These include a value-based fee primer, practical ideas and tools to facilitate conversations between clients and law firms on how to improve the value of legal services, and numerous case studies showing how companies such as General Electric and Johnson & Johnson have successfully used AFAs in complex cases and transactions.

In addition to making use of tools such as those provided by the ACC, clients have begun to make much greater use of their companies' procurement departments to drive down price. Altman Weil found that 19 per cent of the chief legal officers (CLOs) that it surveyed had involved their procurement teams in law firm selection. This is a fairly recent phenomenon and an erosion of the much prized relationship-based approach to law firm selection. There is a trend for clients to conduct panel reviews which decrease the number of firms acting for each client. The winning firms secure a much larger piece of the client pie (or sometimes obtain an exclusive mandate, as was the case when Tyco handed an exclusive remit to Eversheds). But the coveted places on the panel are often granted in exchange for the agreement of creative fee arrangements, such as flat-rate retainers and fixed-price matters. Case Study 3 contains an interview with a legal procurement manager, which illustrates the ways in which procurement teams wring concessions from law firms.

It would be wrong to give the impression that all clients are paragons of commercial virtue and expert at pricing and managing matters. In his strongly worded article 'In Defence of the Billable Hour'[8] Mark Brandon of Motive Legal Consulting pours cold water on the notion that all in-house counsel know how to run AFAs. "In my experience, in-house lawyers are just as diverse a bunch as private practice lawyers; and they are just as capable of being arrogant, pompous, unworldly, narrow-minded and illogical as the next man (or woman)... It often suits the legal press to canonise in-house lawyers and some commentators seem to credit them with the wisdom of Solomon. Nonetheless, that should not sway us from the reality that the client market is highly diverse and generally unequipped to make a detailed determination of every aspect of the service they're buying."

Brandon's doubts are echoed by Jim Diamond, a costs lawyer who compiled the survey of lawyers' charge-out rates reported by *The Lawyer* previously. He concludes that in-house lawyers are not as effective at managing their legal fees as they think they are. "Every in-house lawyer thinks they're an expert in cost management, but it looks like a lot are just paying lip service," he says. "Only a few are actually backing up what they say and managing to drive costs down."

Some in-house lawyers (as reported in Case Study 3) will know their limitations and opt to play it safe with hourly rates, while others may make unreasonable fee demands of their outside counsel. Numbers of high profile and well-resourced big spenders, such as Pfizer and DuPont, or collectives of lawyer interest groups such as the ACC, are making constructive and tangible attacks on the hourly rate. And where they have led, others are following.

Economic pressures

The principal reason that clients have become so active in seeking AFAs is that their own legal budgets have been slashed in the wake of the global financial collapse. Research from Hildebrandt Baker Robbins (quoted in the *Legal Week* survey) indicates that worldwide legal spend on law firms contracted by five to six per cent in 2010. According to Altman Weil, a full 29 per cent of the CLOs surveyed intended to decrease their use of outside counsel in the next 12 months.

This makes grim reading indeed for law firms. The turmoil in the Eurozone has been well publicised. Influential think tank, the Organisation for Economic Co-operation and Development, recently commented that, in the UK "the recovery paused in end-2010 and growth is projected to remain weak in 2011".[9] The situation is mirrored in the US where, at the end of July 2011, Washington finally reached an agreement to raise the debt ceiling after months of wrangling. But even this did not cause stock markets to rally, as fundamentals remained weak.

Australia, despite suffering from major natural disasters in early 2011, has largely escaped the economic gloom and provides a welcome exception (perhaps explaining the rush by several international law firms to secure a greater share of that market). Unsurprisingly, 47 per cent of managing partners surveyed by Winmark in 2011 are predicting further economic stagnation whilst partners in the City of London are generally reporting patchy work levels.

With no sign of economic pressures abating in most jurisdictions, law firms can expect to see clients continuing to push for better value and alternative fees.

Technological advances

The acknowledged guru in the field of legal technology is Professor Richard Susskind. It will astonish no one that he expects there will be much greater reliance on IT-based legal systems in the future, and that this will drive a trend away from bespoke work to more commoditized legal services. In his seminal book *The End of Lawyers?*[10] Susskind surveys the changes wrought over the past decade and makes predictions for the future.

One of Susskind's influences is Professor Clayton Christensen of Harvard Business School, whose work on disruptive technologies is adapted by Susskind for the legal profession. Susskind foresees a number of disruptive technologies impacting the way that lawyers work and charge for their services in future. The most relevant disruptive technologies for the purposes of this report are:

- Automated document assembly;
- An electronic legal market place (such as law firm price comparison sites and electronic auctions);
- Online legal guidance;
- Legal open-sourcing (such as Wikipedia or a specialist legal equivalent);
- Closed legal communities (such as the ACC described above, or Winmark's CLO Programme); and
- Workflow and project management (more information on these topics is available in Chapter 6 and Case study 1).

Many of these technologies are already nascent and have made further inroads into the legal market since Susskind's book was published in 2008. Susskind himself quotes William Gibson's line, "The future has already arrived. It's just not evenly distributed yet."

A further consequence of internet technology and electronic communications is that firms and clients can divide matters into constituent parts and outsource or multi-source elements. This is discussed more fully in the section on outsourcing below.

Susskind believes that there will still be a role for the trusted adviser but his analysis concludes that lawyers are too readily inclined to believe that what they do needs to be bespoke, when in fact clients may appreciate a cheaper, faster and more accessible standard product (at least some of the time).

When it comes to pricing legal work, Susskind concludes that due to the information revolution produced by the internet, "The old system, one that has allowed lawyers to under-perform and overcharge, is to be replaced by a new model, under which all law firms will be subject to far greater scrutiny and competition – on availability, price, performance and client satisfaction. The free market is coming soon to the world of law."

Liberalisation of law firm regulation

Long-awaited regulatory reform arrives in the UK in October 2011, when the Legal Services Act 2007 finally comes into force. The Legal Services Act will permit law firms to form alternative business structures (ABS). One of the key reforms is that, in future, law firms could be owned and managed by non-lawyers, such as insurance companies, banks, estate agents and supermarkets. Indeed, the Legal Services Act is sometimes dubbed 'Tesco Law' although whether that particular supermarket enters the fray remains to be seen. Law firms will also be able to seek external investment and float on the stock market.

Nick Jarrett-Kerr describes the rationale behind the reforms as "a blatant attempt to apply a greater degree of market forces to a professional services sector which has been seen as traditionally monopolistic and restrictive".

One UK firm, Irwin Mitchell, has already announced that it plans to float under the new regime. *The Lawyer*[11] reported that the firm, which is currently 22nd in the UK rankings by turnover, and hitherto known for its personal injury work, intends to build a "£50m war chest" to enable it to fund growth through acquisition and to "go head-to-head with mid-tier corporate firms."

Most of the rest of the profession has chosen to maintain a studied silence. Neil Rose of Legal Futures accuses lawyers of burying their heads in the sand. He comments: "For many years lawyers have largely ignored the oncoming storm, but... they can do so no longer. To generalise, lawyers are second movers and there is a great deal of 'wait and see' going on at the moment, although the profession's history is littered with moments when it has let others take the initiative and eat its breakfast."[12]

More interest has been expressed by certain large, non-legal companies, notably the Co-operative Group, known as 'the Co-op' – the UK's largest mutual retailer (owned by six million consumers rather than shareholders). Two divisions of the Co-op (Co-operative Legal Services and Co-operative Financial Services) look likely to team up to see if they can offer legal services from their bank branches. The Co-op is also expected to bring in-house a significant volume of personal injury claim work that it presently outsources.

In other recent moves, many high street firms acting for consumers have banded together in umbrella organisations, such as Quality Solicitors, Face2Face Solicitors and High Street Lawyer.com. Such groups are positioning themselves to take advantage of external investment opportunities.

The UK is not the first country to allow alternative business structures. Australia, Belgium and the Netherlands, for example, already do so. Australia's Slater & Gordon, a plaintiff law firm with 900 staff and 40 offices across Australia, rose to international prominence when it became the first law firm to float on the Australian stock exchange in 2007.

It seems that the UK is unlikely to be the last country to allow alternative business structures either. In April this year, the American Bar Association launched a white paper to discuss the potential for permitting alternative business structures across the US (currently only permitted in the District of Columbia).[13]

Nick Jarrett-Kerr concludes that, "Not every firm will want or need to become an ABS, but every firm does need to look very closely at the competitive pressures it will face." The unavoidable inference is that the introduction of ABS can only increase rather than diminish the importance of pricing for law firms.

Legal process outsourcing

There has been much hype in the press about legal process outsourcing (LPO) where a client, or indeed a law firm, farms out work (outsources) to another law firm or to a legal support services company. Very often this outsourcing is to a low-cost jurisdiction, in which case it may be referred to as offshoring.

Altman Weil found that 15 per cent of the CLOs it surveyed for its 2010 report were using offshoring for at least some of their legal work.

Two factors propelling the growth of offshoring are economic pressures and technological advances, as previously described.

The attraction of offshoring is that it enables clients to obtain essential but more routine legal services at a fraction of the fee that they would pay in their home jurisdictions. India has been a particularly popular location due to its plentiful supply of inexpensive, well-educated, English speakers trained in English common law. Technological advances have made the logistics of offshoring workable. Documents can be shared over the internet or emailed to India for review as easily as they can be sent to the office next door.

Forrester Research has forecast that revenues from LPO will grow from around $640m in 2010 to over $4bn by 2015. These forecasts have been challenged but even the much more conservative Evalueserve (itself an LPO provider) has predicted that LPO will reach nearly $1bn in the same time frame, which would represent just over one per cent of the US legal market at that time. This indicates that LPO is making slower inroads into the legal industry than it is into other sectors such as banking and finance, where it is expected to reach ten to 12 per cent by 2014.[14] As usual, the reason given for this lag is the conservative nature of the legal profession.

Whilst LPO is not yet really taking significant volumes of work away from domestic law firms, clients are increasingly wise to the possibility of outsourcing work or of splitting matters and taking the more administrative elements of transactions away from their traditional law firms. This alone may serve to make domestic law firms price more keenly and consider more closely how they resource and manage their matters.

Impact of AFAs

This chapter has shown that while hourly rates remain the chief means of calculating legal fees, their dominance is being eroded year on year, as AFAs become more established and clients and law firms become more adept at using them.

A number of significant factors – including client activism, economic pressures, technological advances, liberalisation of legal services and growth of LPO – are combining to mount a sustained attack on hourly rate billing and to keep fee structures high on the agenda. This is borne out by Altman Weil's findings that 72 per cent of managing partners place pricing in their top three areas for strategic focus.

However, making a success of AFAs requires a whole new approach to taking instructions, scoping work, planning, resourcing and budgeting a matter and agreeing fees through negotiation. As was shown in Chapter 1, some firms have launched into providing AFAs without preparing the groundwork and are suffering as a result. Chapters 4 to 10 address those issues.

References

1. 'Crunch-busting magic circle fees up by half', Andrew Pugh, *The Lawyer*, 20 September 2010, available online at http://www.thelawyer.com

2. 'Magic circle' is commonly taken to refer to the five leading UK headquartered law firms (currently Allen & Overy, Clifford Chance, Freshfields Bruckhaus Deringer, Linklaters and Slaughter and May).
3. All references in this chapter to the Winmark 2011 report are to the *Winmark Looking Glass Report: The Legal World on its Future*, Winmark, London 2011, which surveyed 124 general counsel and legal directors, 57 managing partners and 18 marketing directors
4. All references in this chapter to the *Legal Week* report are to the *Legal Week* Intelligence *Client Satisfaction Report 2010*, *Legal Week* Intelligence, December 2010. This comprises telephone interviews and online and postal questionnaires involving over 900 companies across a wide range of sectors and geographies, but with a greater emphasis on UK and Europe
5. All references in this chapter to Altman Weil are to the 'Chief Legal Officer Survey 2010'
6. ACC is the Association of Corporate Counsel. Its web address is http://www.acc.com. The ACC has been very active in advocating value pricing and has launched the ACC Value Challenge. Many materials are available on the ACC website free of charge
7. All references in this chapter to the Winmark 2010 report are to the *Winmark Looking Glass Report: The Legal World on its Future*, Winmark, London 2010, which surveyed 81 General Counsel, 56 Managing Partners and 23 Marketing Directors
8. 'In Defence of the Billable Hour', Mark Brandon, Motive Legal Consulting, London, April 2011
9. Organisation for Economic Co-operation and Development, 25 May 2011
10. *The End of Lawyers? Rethinking the Nature of Legal Services*, Richard Susskind, Oxford University Press, Oxford, 2008
11. 'Irwin Mitchell: we'll float and take on the mid tier', Katy Dowell, *The Lawyer*, 25th April 2011, http://www.thelawyer.com
12. 'Tesco law – not the big bang, but it will change the future of legal services', Neil Rose of Legal Futures writing in the *Guardian* newspaper on 25th March 2011
13. 'ABA opens door for America to embrace to embrace alternative business structures', as reported by Legal Futures, http://www.legalfutures.co.uk on 5th April 2011
14. All figures quoted in this paragraph are taken from *Offshoring Times*, 'Future of LPO', http://www.offshoringtimes.com

Chapter 3: Alternative fees – Risks and how to avoid them

"In the struggle for survival, the fittest win out at the expense of their rivals because they succeed in adapting themselves best to their environment." Charles Darwin

Risk 1: Alternative fees are not as profitable as hourly rates

Many law firm partners argue that hourly rate billing is a time-honoured, straightforward and profitable way to bill clients. Those who have tried to encourage partners to adopt alternatives complain that 'it's hard to argue with millionaires'.

With equity partners at Slaughter and May, Freshfields Bruckhaus Deringer, Allen & Overy and Linklaters taking home well over £1m per year, a certain amount of complacency is bound to set in. The mantra, 'if it ain't broke, don't fix it' reverberates through many currently successful legal practices.

By contrast, those firms which have dabbled with AFAs have often found them to be deeply unprofitable – when the amount of a pre-agreed fixed fee or cap is compared with the amount of time on the clock. This would be typical of firms in categories B or C of the universal law firm fee continuum, described in Chapter 1.

Response: Alternative fees can be highly profitable

Chapter 2 showed that while hourly billing remains law firms' preferred charging method, client activism and other forces such as economic pressures, technological advances, regulatory easing and growth of LPO have mounted a sustained and increasing attack on the viability of firms relying purely on hourly rate billing.

Although some firms have managed to maintain, or even increase, profits during the economic downturn, a closer examination often reveals that the increased profits were the result of cost-cutting measures, rather than revenue growth. This was the case with Debevoise & Plimpton in 2010. The firm's profit per equity partner rose 11 per cent to an enviable $2.06m, but on the back of a two per cent decline in revenue (which itself followed a 12 per cent revenue decline the previous year).[1]

In pure financial terms, cost-cutting is an essential element of profit management in any business. In law firms it tends to mean redundancies and carries a concomitant human cost, drain on morale and diminution of capability. In many firms, reductions in head count have been made at all levels of the human resources pyramid, from support staff through to equity partners. In the longer term, no business can sustain profit growth through cost-cutting measures alone.

It is true that many law firms' first attempts at AFAs are not very profitable. This is because most firms begin with individual partners making piecemeal attempts at offering AFAs, often as a result of client pressure, and generally without the necessary financial understanding or business tools to accurately predict the likely cost of conducting the matter to the firm. The lawyers also lack the skills and tools to ensure that the matter is completed within the pre-agreed budget.

The remaining chapters of this report will demonstrate how lawyers can create accurate matter budgets which reflect the cost to the firm of performing the matter and how to negotiate fees which both deliver the firm's desired profit margin and provide value and satisfaction to the client.

Firms which have successfully adopted AFAs have found that in some cases they make greater profits than they would have done employing hourly rates. This could be for a number of reasons such as:

- The firms have won work which they would not have obtained if they had not been able to offer AFAs, either through gaining panel places (sometimes on an exclusive basis) or a greater share of wallet from an existing client;
- The discipline of working with AFAs has forced the firms to adopt more efficient approaches which save costs – for example by automating and standardising more of their processes and documentation. Unlike headcount reductions, which are made in the short term to cut staff costs without simultaneous innovations, these efficiency measures increase rather than reduce the firm's capacity to handle more matters; and
- Some AFAs can themselves be very lucrative. On business-critical matters, clients may agree to holdback and bonus arrangements, whereby the firm can earn a significant uplift on what it would have earned by billing only for time on the clock. Case Study 2 provides examples of how holdback arrangements can work in practice.

However, none of these benefits will accrue unless senior management teams invest in building budgeting and negotiating capability within their firms.

Risk 2: Alternative fees transfer risk to the law firm

Cost plus billing methods (where the fee reflects the number of hours actually worked) place all the risk of a transaction being more complicated than was first anticipated squarely on the client's shoulders. The fee will be what it will be. This places lawyers in an unusually sheltered position, which they are understandably loathe to sacrifice.

In contrast, AFAs do transfer some of the risk from the client to the law firm. Lawyers' profit margins may be eroded or even vanish if they work more hours than expected, if a transaction aborts, or a case is lost.

Response: The budgeting and negotiating process can enable firms and clients to find acceptable ways to share and manage risk

Many dispassionate observers would argue that it is entirely appropriate that law firms should take some risk in the matters that they handle. After all, they are the purported experts in the field. As such, they should be far better placed than their clients to estimate the likely cost of their services, and to predict the stages through which the matter will need to progress, or hurdles which will need to be overcome. Indeed, clients often speak approvingly of those law firms which have 'some skin in the game'. Clients think that such risk sharing 'keeps their lawyers honest' as they work in common cause to bring their matters to successful conclusions as efficiently as possible.

Law firms need not bear all the risk of a matter when working with AFAs. Firms and clients are not restricted to agreeing such binary outcomes. The beauty of AFAs is that both parties agree bespoke fee structures which satisfy their mutual requirements. The firm needs to agree a scope of work with the client, making sure to clarify the extent of its remit and the client's objectives.

The firm will then need to prepare a detailed matter plan, which sets out the expected stages of the matter, how the work will be staffed and how many hours each stage is expected to require of each staff member. Matter plans are described in more detail in Chapter 5 and a template is provided in Appendix 1 of this report.

Having created a matter plan, the firm can use a budget calculator of the kind supplied in Appendix 2 to establish its baseline, expected costing for the matter. Finally, the law firm will adapt these figures in the light of other factors, such as historic charges for similar matters, urgency or importance of the matter and the client's working style. It is vital that the law firm shares the scope of work with the client and confirms with the client where the priorities lie.

Agreeing the scope also involves defining what is 'out of scope'. There may be times when a matter deviates from the scope, despite the best efforts of the lawyer. This might be if the client genuinely changes or expands its instructions to the firm (despite having had the scope clearly explained and agreed). Or, if events beyond the control of either party (such as insolvency of a key supplier, a regulatory investigation or the dismissal of a senior employee) serve to create new work streams which had been outside both parties' contemplation when the matter began. The engagement letter should include a clear protocol for both parties to adhere to if the instructions need to change part way through a matter. If instructions change at the client's discretion then it is only right and proper that the client should bear the additional cost. The only grounds for objection that clients could have would be if:

- The client felt that the additional work was foreseeable and that the law firm had erred in not explaining the proper scope of the work to them in the first place; or
- The law firm failed to acknowledge explicitly and in a timely fashion that the matter had gone out of scope.

Having planned the matter and provided a detailed and agreed scope of work in an engagement letter, the law firm will already have gone a long way towards de-risking the matter. The more practice that the law firm has had in creating matter budgets and matter plans, the more accurate these will be and the lower the risk to the firm.

Pricing an AFA is not necessarily pegged purely to the law firm's costs (although firms would always be advised to calculate the likely cost of performing a matter before agreeing to a fee). The law firm and client may agree to factor in other considerations of value, such as speed of delivery (as discussed in Chapter 9 and Case Study 2).

Alternatively the firm may have agreed that it will earn a bonus if certain targets are met or the client is particularly satisfied. The firm may agree that the fee increases with a successful result and decreases if the matter does not achieve the client's aims. Here the firm openly takes on risk for matters that are not entirely within its control. The reciprocal of risk is reward. Firms that take on this kind of risk should be well positioned to argue that their willingness to share in the downside of a matter entitles them to share in the upside too.

Working on the basis of an AFA will involve an element of up-front fee negotiation with the client. This need not be a combative experience. It is likely to begin with exploratory dialogue which shapes the scope of work. Armed with an agreed scope, the expected cost for performing the work, and with a fine appreciation of how it will add value for the client, the law firm will be in a good position to negotiate a favourable fee arrangement.

Risk 3: Alternative fees will lead to commoditization and erode premiums

Offering fixed fees is resisted by some firms on the basis that it is the first step on the road to commoditization. Once something has been defined as a commodity, competitive forces exert price pressure and from there it is a downward spiral.

Some, higher volume types of legal work, such as conveyancing and personal injury, are already considered to be commodity items. Profit margins are as low as two per cent for providers of commoditized legal services. Unsurprisingly, lawyers who pride themselves on delivering a tailored, high quality and intelligent service, which is priced on a matter-by-matter basis (depending on the number of hours worked) are very reluctant to open the door to new methods of pricing and providing their work which could erode the premiums that they currently command.

Response: Premium work will continue to command premium fees, but the definition of premium will evolve and firms will need to adapt in order to thrive

Some previously bespoke legal work may become commoditized. The term is used quite loosely here to refer to work which has become fairly routine and as a result commands low margin. The commoditization of some types of legal work applied before the advent of the internet but the relentless march of technology has exacerbated the trend.

As discussed in Chapter 2, disruptive technologies including automated document assembly, legal open-sourcing and social networking sites provide clients with access to standard documents, precedents and advice for which they would previously have paid top dollar. What once was cutting-edge advice becomes trite law. A proprietary tax structure becomes ubiquitous.

If a service has become a commodity, there is no use in denying it. Firms that bury their heads in the sand will find that others are willing to offer the services at commodity prices. Clients, who are less taken than lawyers with the notion of firms providing them with a totally bespoke service, or starting with a blank sheet of paper, will flock to providers who can provide consistent, reliable, timely and cheap services for a certain price.

Commoditization of some types of legal work does not presage the commoditization of all types of legal work. Whilst clients will not pay to reinvent the wheel once they have realised that they don't have to, they will continue to pay substantial sums for expert advice, drafting, negotiation and advocacy, coupled with efficient transaction and case management. Allen & Overy and Linklaters are two excellent examples of firms which command absolutely premium prices for their mainstream work but have recognised that elements of the service that they provide have become commoditized.

Linklaters' response to this phenomenon was the launch of its Blue Flag service. Allen & Overy followed with its Online Services. It is perhaps no coincidence that both firms have strong banking practices. The banking sector long ago conceded the benefits of standardisation with the adoption of the master agreement of the International Swaps and Derivatives Association (ISDA).

To take one example from the suite of services provided by each firm on a subscription basis, Allen & Overy now provides a service called CSAnalytics, which enables clients to "manage credit and legal risk for derivatives trades relating to the taking of collateral under standard ISDA documentation".

Linklaters offers a Term Sheet Generator which "helps bankers produce term sheets more accurately and more quickly. Fully interactive, it also contains an embedded advisory capability and directs clients to the most relevant information for structuring their deals".

To many law firms it is still unthinkable that they should de-mystify the art of legal practice by admitting that it is capable of standardisation and by making their crown jewels widely available at modest cost. Yet Allen & Overy and Linklaters both stand testament to the success of the strategy. If anything, it binds clients closer to those firms and has not inhibited them from achieving net profit of £507m for Linklaters and £388m for Allen & Overy, in 2010.

The ability to face up to and adapt to changes in the market place will distinguish long-term law firm winners and losers. In the words of Charles Darwin, "In the struggle for survival, the fittest win out at the expense of their rivals because they succeed in adapting themselves best to their environment."[2]

Risk 4: Alternative fee structures are not compatible with billable hours targets

When billing by the hour, the only ways to increase profits are to bill more hours, increase rates or cut costs – hence the widespread use of billable hours targets.

On the other hand, alternative fee structures are predicated upon efficient working practices. Matters completed in fewer hours are more profitable than those which take up more time. Firms are not paid for the number of hours worked but for the results that they achieve. However, the majority of fee earners are still appraised (and sometimes remunerated) on the basis of hitting onerous billable hours targets. The two appear incompatible.

Response: Align rewards with strategy

AFAs and billable hours targets are indeed incompatible. The simple answer is that firms which embrace AFAs need to scrap their billable hours targets. At least as far as partners are concerned, productivity can be assessed in other ways, such as fees earned (as is the case in DMH Stallard, the subject of Case Study 1). This means that partners are not rewarded for hours worked that are not ultimately recovered. Partners can also be measured on their profit margins, which are much more meaningful markers of their contribution to their firm's finances than the hours that they work.

Use of such metrics encourages partners to take on high-margin work and to price in accordance with the firm's pricing policies, rather than just pursuing new business for the sake of it without thought to whether it is worthwhile business. Partners can similarly be judged on the proportion of their matters which come in on time and on budget. This will be an indicator of whether they are honing their budgeting and negotiating skills and using the business tools provided by the law firm. It may also be a good proxy for whether they are conducting matters profitably. All lawyers can be appraised on client satisfaction. This is a much better long-term predictor of the continued success of the firm than how hard everybody works.

These measures can be summarised as aligning the firm's recognition and reward systems with its strategy, which is examined in Chapter 12. Firms that abandon billable hours targets may also reap the additional bonus of more contented and fulfilled staff, who no longer feel that they are slaves to such targets. The resultant slowdown in fee earner attrition will also bring financial benefits to the firm.

References

1. 'Debevoise revenues slip again but partner profits climb to $2m', Nate Raymond, *Legal Week*, 23 February 2011, http://www.legalweek.com
2. Commonly attributed to Charles Darwin

Chapter 4: Understanding law firm financial data – a pre-requisite for successful budgeting and negotiation

"Turnover is vanity, profit is sanity but cash is king." Traditional

HAVING EXAMINED the many circumstances in which lawyers are likely to find themselves in need of budgeting and negotiating skills this report has moved on to explore the increasing pressure to adopt AFAs, exerted on firms by clients and market forces. It has addressed the reasons that firms might be reluctant to adopt AFAs and showed how astute budgeting and negotiating tactics could go a long way to alleviate the risks associated with their use.

The greater the proportion of matters undertaken on the basis of AFAs, the more vital it becomes for law firms to approach fee structuring on a rational basis. The ongoing viability of the law firm will hinge on lawyers understanding the cost of conducting any piece of work and the expected profit margin to be achieved. Such understanding is crucial in order to maintain attractive levels of profit for the equity partners and to provide cash to fund the business.

It seems likely that for some time to come, at least a proportion of matters will continue to be priced on the basis of hourly rates. But as virtually all clients look to manage their legal spend tightly, firms will seldom be able to recover 100 per cent of their standard rates or all of the time recorded by fee earners on each matter. Those lawyers will often be asked to provide discounts to their standard hourly rates for favoured clients and may also be asked to slash final bills because they are just too steep for clients to swallow. Here, lawyers will need to understand their firm's finances so that they do not unwittingly wipe out all their profit by agreeing to unsustainable discounts.

Partners in law firms can currently expect to receive a wealth of financial information, but this slew of data often leaves them feeling overwhelmed and yet under informed at the same time. Automated accounting systems produce reams of information but it is not necessarily marshalled in a way which helps lawyers to price client matters. Formal training on the meaning of accounting information is also often limited.

This chapter therefore sets out to explain the critical elements of law firm financial data, which all lawyers need to understand in order to price their work effectively. It begins by defining the two most important criteria upon which the financial health of a law firm can be judged: profits and cash. It will then describe how lawyers should read their firm's accounts to ascertain its profitability and cash position. Finally, it will explain why and how lawyers should delve beneath the surface of their firm's data to examine departmental, individual and matter information, in order to create realistic budgets and fee targets for the matters that they are personally responsible for. This report does not purport to be an exhaustive guide to accounting in law firms. Rather, it sets out to provide fee earners with the tools and understanding that they need in order to prepare matter estimates, negotiate fees with their clients and work within their budgets.

This report is intended to provide guidance both for individual lawyers who are determined to improve their own budgeting and negotiating skills; and also for firm and department leaders who need to devise budgeting and negotiating strategies to be adopted by their firms, or who are charged with creating useful management information, training and systems for their lawyers.

In order to illustrate the points to be made in Chapters 4 and 5, simplified financial figures have been created for an imaginary firm called Hypothetical UK LLP. The accounts are shown in Table 1. The firm is representative of a top-50 UK law firm. The figures are realistic for a firm of this size but are not based on any particular firm and are not designed to represent an ideal. Throughout Chapters 4 and 5, references are made to the accounts of Hypothetical UK LLP to clarify and bring to life the topics under discussion. The accounts have been prepared in a simplified version of the format which would be adopted by a UK LLP as this is rapidly becoming the structure of choice for major UK law firms. The UK LLP structure is different from that of a US LLP, apparently having more in common with a US LLC. Accounts for traditional UK partnerships and US firms may be drawn up differently but the principles discussed in these chapters remain the same.

The significance of profit

Equity partners in law firms are rewarded for their contribution to their firms by means of profit share. As a result profit margins and profits per equity partner (PEP) are the most talked about measures of law firm success. These days, firm PEP figures are published and widely discussed, which heaps pressure on firm leaders to push for ever increasing levels. Even at the top echelons, the degree of profitability of law firms varies enormously.

Take, for example, the two international law firm behemoths Clifford Chance and Linklaters, which were ranked first and second largest firms in the UK by turnover, in 2010. Clifford Chance's turnover for the year was £1.197bn whereas Linklaters' was £1.183bn. These figures are very close but a huge disparity emerges in their net profit, with Clifford Chance achieving £350m compared to £507m at Linklaters. In other words, Linklaters scored a profit margin of 43 per cent against Clifford Chance's 29 per cent, off the back of very similar turnover figures. This report does not set out to explain the divergence in the results of these two particular firms. Rather, the point being made here is that lawyers focus exclusively on turnover (fees) at their peril.

Profit is a much more important measure as equity partners are rewarded in accordance with profits rather than turnover. In the case in point, PEP at Clifford Chance was a very substantial £933,000 in 2010. But at its rivals, Linklaters, PEP was £1,214,000 – nearly a third as much again.[1]

Calculating firm profit and PEP

Profit

The profit and loss account shows the profit or loss made by the whole firm for the year. In the case of UK LLPs, this will take the form of a public document which must be registered at Companies House. A sample profit and loss account is provided for Hypothetical UK LLP in Table 1. The top line of the profit and loss account shows the firm's turnover for the year. Turnover refers to fees earned. This figure, although it may look impressive, is not very informative when examined in isolation.

Balance sheet		
Fixed assets	£30,000,000	
Current assets		
Debtors and WIP on accruals basis	£80,000,000	
Cash	£5,000,000	
Amounts due from members	£15,000,000	
	£100,000,000	
Current liabilities		
Bank overdraft	£15,000,000	
Loans	£10,000,000	
Creditors	£5,000,000	
Tax	£10,000,000	
Accruals	£10,000,000	
	£50,000,000	
Net current assets (current assets less current liabilities)		£50,000,000
Net assets attributable to members (total assets less current liabilities)		£80,000,000
Represented by:		
Loans and other debts due to members		£20,000,000
Equity		£60,000,000
		£80,000,000
Total members interests		
Amounts due from members		-£15,000,000
Loans due to members		£20,000,000
Equity		£60,000,000
		£65,000,000

Profit and loss account	
Income	£200,000,000
Staff costs	-£70,000,000
Other expenses	-£65,000,000
Operating profit	£65,000,000
Net interest payable/receivable	-£500,000
Profit before members' remuneration	£64,500,000
Members' remuneration	£14,500,000
Net profit	£40,000,000

Key metrics	
Operating profit margin	32.5%
Total number of partners	180
Equity partners	100
Salaried partners	80
Members' remuneration	£14,500,000
Net profit for distribution to Equity Partners	£40,000,000
Profit per equity partner	£400,000
Gearing	1:5
Debtors and WIP in months	5

Table 1: Hypothetical UK LLP – Simplified accounts and key metrics

To make sense of a profit and loss account it is necessary to look at the expenditure required to achieve the turnover. In the profit and loss account, the expenses of running the business are subtracted from the turnover in order to achieve the net profit or bottom line. The only ways to increase profit are either to increase turnover or to reduce expenses, or a combination of both.

For many years, the accepted wisdom has been that law firms should aspire to the 'rule of thirds'. That is, that firm turnover should be allocated in broadly equal tranches to salary costs, other overheads and operating profit. This is the rule that applies at Hypothetical UK LLP, where salary and other overhead costs account for approximately one third of the firm's turnover each, leaving an operating profit of one third of turnover.

In practice, there are wide variations in the margins actually achieved by law firms with the very top performing firms achieving profit margins of over 50 per cent.

The Law Management Section of the Law Society of England & Wales (LMS) produces an annual financial benchmarking survey. In the latest survey from 2010,[2] it is apparent that most firms in the UK can only dream of achieving such results, with profit margins starting at 14 per cent.

PEP

This figure is derived from the profit and loss account and is simply the net profit of the firm divided by the number of equity partners. Controversy rages about how to define the best measure of law firm success but PEP is certainly a contender and is probably the most cited statistic in the legal press. It is also the figure most likely to be scrutinised by potential lateral hires to a partnership. PEP figures will be very strongly affected by the proportion of salaried partners to equity partners in a firm.

Not all firms have salaried partners. In those that do, the salaries of these highly paid employees will be likely to reduce the available PEP. The formal profit and loss account is also unlikely to reflect the true cost of the equity partners to the firm. If a notional salary for equity partners is deducted from the net profits of the firm then the profit margins can be expected to be reduced commensurately. When trying to judge the relative profitability of a variety of firms by comparing their PEP figures, it is worth bearing in mind the ratio of equity to salaried partners and re-calibrating the figures to allow for a notional salary for the equity partners.

While firms are often ranked by profitability and PEP, and firm leaders must set annual profit targets upon which hourly rates are likely to be set, firm profit targets are blunt instruments on which to base matter budgets. This chapter will later outline the actionable data which lawyers should refer to in setting matter budgets, but will first examine the importance of cash.

The importance of cash

Law firms run on cash, hence the old adage, "turnover is vanity, profit is sanity but cash is king". Salaries, overheads and drawings cannot be paid – without resorting to expensive and increasingly hard to obtain bank finance and overdrafts – unless underpinned by cash. The secrets of good working capital management and credit control form the subject of entire books. For the purposes of this report, the key point to emphasise is that good working capital management requires lawyers to issue regular bills which are swiftly paid in full.

It is much easier for lawyers to issue bills regularly if there is an agreed billing schedule with the client and if both lawyer and client have agreed in advance the likely quantum of each bill. Furthermore, bills are paid much faster if they have been agreed in advance with the client, who simply sends them on directly to their accounts team with an instruction to pay.

Bills which have spiralled out of control are likely to lie festering; first on the desk of the lawyer, who has to pluck up the courage to send out the offending item, or must undertake the unprofitable task of writing off time before submitting the bill. Then next, on the desk of the client, who will delay the unpleasant task of confronting the lawyer over the bill but will certainly not pay it in the meantime. In order to reach agreement over the bill with the client in advance, it will be necessary for the lawyer to engage in budgeting and negotiating activity, both of which are the subject of the subsequent chapters of this book.

Understanding the firm's cash position

A firm's balance sheet will show its assets and liabilities at a particular point in time. A simplified balance sheet for Hypothetical UK LLP is shown in Table 1. It is a snapshot and quickly becomes out of date. Most of the information in a balance sheet is not relevant to lawyers' day to day practice.

Lawyers should focus on the line items relating to debtors and work in progress. These figures are indicative of the firm's working capital management. The three key measures are:

- Cash;
- Work in progress (WIP) – work which has been undertaken but not yet billed; and
- Debtors – work which has been billed but not yet paid.

WIP and debtors may be described in monetary units or in the number of days it takes a law firm to get paid. When combined, WIP and debtors are referred to as 'lock-up'. This represents the total number of days from receiving instructions to receiving payment.

In order to judge the impact of working practices on the firm's profits and cash position, it is more instructive to focus on the impact of WIP and debtor days on profits and cash flow than to study a balance sheet. A worked example for Hypothetical UK LLP is provided in Table 2. This follows the fortunes of the firm over a three-year period.

The first year's figures are based on the profit and loss account and balance sheet which have already been provided; except that, for the purposes of Table 2, the firm finances all its WIP and debtors through bank loans. In the first year, the firm has revenues of £200m. It has a total lock-up of five months. The firm pays bank interest at eight per cent while it waits for clients to pay, which results in profit before tax of £58m.

In the second year, the firm increases its revenues by ten per cent to £220m. Its lock-up period remains the same. The firm's profits increase to £65m. The section of Table 2 labelled 'cash flow' shows that there is an extra £8m locked-up compared with the previous year and that the firm has received £57m in cash.

In year three, the firm's managing partner launches 'strategy A', an aggressive pursuit of new business, and revenues increase by a further ten per cent to £242m Unfortunately, in the effort to maximise revenues, the firm loosens its grip on working capital management and lock-up now increases to an average of nine months, with disastrous consequences for the firm's cash position.

At the end of the year, the managing partner reviews the strategy again and realises that the firm would actually have been better off following 'strategy B'. Under this, the firm's workload would have been similar to year two, but it would have offered a five per cent discount to clients in return for the clients agreeing to strict payment terms. These terms would have led to work being paid for within two months of instructions being received. In this scenario, the firm's financing costs would have reduced from £7m to £3m. Although the firm's operating profit would have been lower than in year two, its profit before tax would have been equally high and its cash position would have been boosted enormously. This somewhat exaggerated parable illustrates the importance of good cash control.

	Year 1	Year 2	Strategy A Year 3	Strategy B Year 3
Assumptions				
WIP + debtors in months	5	5	9	2
Interest charges	8%	8%	8%	8%
		(£m)		
Profit and Loss				
Revenue	200	220	242	209
Operating profit	65	72	79	68
Interest	7	7	15	3
Profit before tax	58	65	64	65
Balance sheet				
WIP + debtors	80	88	182	35
Cash flow				
Profit		65	64	65
Change in WIP + debtors		8	94	-53
Cash received		57	-30	118

Table 2: Hypothetical UK LLP – Impact of WIP and debtor days on profits and cash flow

Traps for the unwary

When examining law firm accounts, it is important to be aware of the conventions under which they have been drawn up as these can skew the results considerably. In particular, it is important to be aware that UK firms are obliged to account for fees on an accruals basis whereas US firms prepare their accounts on a cash basis. In simple terms, under cash accounting, fees are only recorded once they have been received and expenses are only recorded once they have been paid. UK firms, however, are required to show expenses that have been incurred, even if they have not yet been paid, along with WIP and bills that have been invoiced, even if payment has not yet been received. Anyone reviewing firm results needs to ensure that they are comparing 'apples with apples' not 'apples with pears'. When a firm accounts on an accruals basis, profits that are not actually available for partners to draw may be shown in the accounts.

Actionable data

The preceding sections of this chapter have shown why profit and cash are the two most important indicators of law firm financial health and have explained how lawyers can track their firm's performance. Firm leaders and finance directors will focus a great deal of energy in pursuing firm-wide profit and cash targets. Practice group heads and individual partners need to translate these targets into meaningful working strategies. The remainder of this chapter examines why knowledge of firm targets and past performance alone, is unlikely to provide individual partners and fee earners with sufficient guidance to enable them to price and manage their work effectively.
It then suggests a variety of alternative measures, which fee earners should take into

account when creating matter budgets or negotiating fees with clients.

Firm-wide data hides a multitude of sins. It is very unusual for all departments or individuals within a firm to be operating at the same level of profitability. Certain categories of work, such as corporate finance, are known to command premium rates, whereas insurance litigation is considered much more of a volume business. And although turnover may be high, profit margins are likely to be squeezed. Even within a given practice area, certain matter types are more profitable than others. If lawyers only see firm-wide data then they really do not have sufficient visibility of the profitability of their own work and the needs of their department.

Lawyers who are endeavouring to create accurate matter budgets, ascertain the cost of performing a matter, or establish the point below which they cannot afford to discount fees would be advised to refer to the sources described in the remainder of this chapter.

Management accounts

Firms commonly produce management accounts on a monthly or quarterly basis for internal consumption. As well as containing up-to-date information, these management accounts will ideally include predictions for the next two or three quarters. In this way, fee earners can spot trends and take action if revenues and profits are deviating from expectations. Whereas UK firms are obliged to prepare their annual accounts on an accruals basis, it is generally much easier for lawyers to understand management accounts that are prepared on the basis of cash accounting. Research has shown that where firms prepare their management accounts on a cash basis, lawyers are better at collecting cash from their clients. Partners are also much less likely to accidentally overdraw profits if management accounts are prepared on a cash basis.

Business plans

It is now widely accepted practice for law firms to prepare business plans for the coming 12 months and beyond. Business plans will be created for the firm as a whole but may also be created for each department and even each partner. A personal business plan can help guide a partner as to the fees and profit margins to be generated personally and can be a very useful benchmark when budgeting and negotiating fees.

Departmental data

Firm and practice group leaders need to see financial returns broken down by department and work stream in order to develop a strategy for the firm and each department, based upon a logical analysis of the strongly performing or growth practice areas. Marketing and business development efforts can be concentrated on those areas of the business which are likely to prove most profitable for the firm.

If certain areas are identified as weak, then action can be taken by the firm's leadership and practice group heads to salvage the situation. This may mean prioritising one type of work or client over another, or overhauling the firm's working methods to render them more efficient and consistent through the introduction of case management systems, automated document production, knowledge sharing, delegation and team composition.

Individual fee earners will produce more realistic budgets for their matters if they are based on departmental targets and historic figures. If certain areas of work or certain clients have been identified as having significant growth potential for the department then this may also inform the negotiating positions that the fee earner adopts in order to win particularly sought after business.

Individual data

Individual fee earners, practice group heads and firm leaders will also need to examine individual financial performance. It will soon become apparent that individual fee earners carrying out similar work for comparable clients achieve very different financial returns. Some lawyers are likely to achieve consistently higher profit margins on their matters than other lawyers. These differences can be ascribed to three principal factors, which are unrelated to the nature of the work carried out or the geographical location of the firm. These are:

- Recorded hours;
- Amount of recovery; and
- Speed of payment.

These three factors are relevant both to firms which charge clients in accordance with time spent and to firms which operate AFAs.

Recorded hours

Few lawyers these days enjoy the luxury and leisure of alcohol-fuelled lunches with clients or Friday afternoons on the golf course. Firms relying on time-based billing are acutely aware of the need to incentivise their lawyers to bill ever increasing numbers of hours. Many firms have set punishing billing targets of over 2,000 hours of recorded time per year, which in reality implies around 3,000 hours per year of work. This equates to a 12-hour working day, five days per week. There are many lawyers working harder than this. Whether or not the firm has billable hours targets, there will always be some lawyers who put in more hours in the office than others. Time in the office does not necessarily equal hours billed or profits generated.

As stated above, there is a common perception that it takes 3,000 hours in the office to generate 2,000 hours of recorded time, but individual experience will vary. The discrepancy between working hours and recorded hours can be accounted for in a number of ways. Lawyers are human beings, not robots, and a certain number of breaks, banter around the water cooler, personal phone calls (or these days, Facebook updates, where permitted by the firm) are to be expected.

More concerning for management is the fact that many lawyers self-censor their time recording and write-off time before it has even been recorded, if they feel that it cannot be charged to the client. Lawyers may feel embarrassed about the time it has taken them to research an established piece of law or to draft a contract because they were having a slow day. In a firm that relies on cost plus billing this self-censorship has a very deleterious impact on potential earnings and should be discouraged. The level of self-censorship will vary between one fee earner and another. It also masks the true number of hours required by a fee earner to complete a matter and will make it harder for a firm to use historic matter information as the basis for estimating fees for further pieces of work.

It is self-evident that lawyers who can minimise their wasted hours will be able to record more time or complete more assignments. In firms which offer AFAs such as fixed fees, it is essential that lawyers work efficiently to ensure that the cost to the firm of conducting the matter does not exceed the fee which will be paid.

Recovery

Once hours have been recorded, the person in charge of drawing up the bill is likely to write off further chunks of time if their gut feeling is that the client will not agree to pay for all the time on the clock. All of this discounting is likely to occur before any conversations with the client have even taken place. Where discounts are given, recovery rates and therefore profits fall.

Table 3 shows how drastically operating profit will be hit where a 20 per cent fee discount is given, but the firm's costs in discharging the matter are not similarly reduced. In this example, while income drops 20 per cent, the operating profit has decreased by over 60 per cent. Many lawyers will agree to charge certain favoured clients on the basis of discounted rates. It is not unusual for clients to secure discounts of ten to 20 per cent for all work performed by the firm.

Pre-agreed discounts do not inhibit clients from demanding further invoice-by-invoice discounts if they are unhappy with the bills that they receive and law firms complain bitterly about being 'clobbered at both ends'. If a lawyer gives away a ten per cent discount on top of an existing 20 per cent one, the firm's profit margins are likely to be very substantially eroded.

What may come as a surprise is the fact that discounts offered by one fee earner will be dramatically different from the discounts offered by the other fee earners in the department. Setting aside differences in clients' negotiating styles and strengths, the variance can be explained as follows: some lawyers understand their firm's finances and recognise the impact of discounts on their firm's profitability better than others. Some lawyers are more self-confident than others and some can demonstrate the value of their work better than others. This is another way of saying that some lawyers are better fee negotiators than others. (Chapters 7 to 10 of this report analyse the negotiation process and provide advice on how to negotiate fees effectively.)

Lawyers are often completely unaware of what their colleagues charge. Many lawyers are still uncomfortable discussing something as personal as money. The problem is exacerbated in firms where personal financial performance is either not monitored or not disseminated widely. In such firms, lawyers set their own fees and discounts in the dark.

Some firms, such as DMH Stallard LLP (see Case Study 1) make personal key performance indicators available to all fee earners on the firm's intranet, but this is still the exception rather than the norm.

Even if a firm is not prepared for such transparency, the firm's leaders should at least be monitoring individual performance in order to be able to appraise and reward desirable behaviour and to guide, train and coach those lawyers who are not obtaining optimum results for the firm. When setting budgets, fee earners have much to learn from the results achieved by their colleagues.

	Standard fee	Discounted fee
Fee	£100,000	£80,000
Costs	£67,500	£67,500
Operating profit	£32,500	£12,500
Loss of profit		62%

Table 3: Impact of 20 per cent fee discount on profit margin

Speed of payment
This refers to the time which elapses between a fee earner receiving instructions and the firm getting paid, as discussed earlier. Issuing invoices is not the end of the story and does not automatically result in the firm getting paid. As shown in Table 2, time and effort devoted to reducing WIP, debtor days and bad debts will pay dividends. It can even be worthwhile for fee earners to offer (carefully calibrated) discounts to clients in return for regular and prompt payments.

Matter data

Matter data needs to be examined for much the same reasons as individual data. The fees charged and profits generated even for outwardly similar matters tend to vary enormously. Lawyers are quick to point out that every matter brings its own complications but the fee differential may not be justifiable to the client, even when the law firm pleads extenuating circumstances.

In addition to all the factors highlighted in the previous section on individual data, other factors which can have a bearing on cost to a firm of carrying out a matter are:

- Resourcing – which fee earners are assigned to the matter;
- Gearing – literally the number of assistants working for each equity partner, but also the proportion of time spent on the matter by assistant solicitors rather than partners;
- Knowledge sharing – to avoid reinventing the wheel; and
- Automation – to streamline document creation.

When firms were able to charge purely on the basis of time on the clock, scant attention was paid to discrepancies between matters as the firm's expected profit margin was hard-wired into the hourly rate. In the current economic environment, clients are under pressure to cut costs and are increasingly well informed about their own historic legal spend on particular matter types. They also possess strong views as to the market price for a given matter. Firms are likely to be forced to write off time if they have operated inefficiently. The imperative to predict matter cost accurately will be even greater for firms operating on the basis of fixed, capped or value fees.

There are valuable lessons to be learned from a firm's historic matter data. Not only will historic matter data help firms to produce sensible matter estimates for future work, it can also be analysed to highlight processes which need to be re-engineered, or people who need to be coached in order to maintain or enhance firm profitability.

Chapter 5 describes how to create a realistic matter budget, which relies in part on making use of the firm's historic matter data.

It is vital that all lawyers understand the importance of profits and cash and know where to look for data that will inform their personal budgeting and negotiating positions. Having read this chapter, lawyers should be able to recognise the shortcomings of data relating to the firm as a whole and why it is important to drill down to departmental, personal and matter data in order to establish personal targets which are aligned with the firm's strategic plan.

Adopting best practice in budgeting and negotiating enormously enhances the speed of bill payment by clients and therefore the firm's cash position, and leads to increased recovery which is converted to profits and cash. Embedding best practice behaviours is discussed in detail in Chapter 12.

References

1. *The Lawyer UK 200 Annual Report* (2010), citing figures for the financial year 2009/10
2. The Law Management Section of the Law Society, 'Financial Benchmarking Survey 2010', The Law Society, London, 2011

Chapter 5: Creating a realistic matter budget

"Can you honestly think of any other purchase decision that is made on the basis of an uncertain outcome, an uncertain price, and an uncertain incidence of when the price has to be paid?" Paul Gilbert

Are budgets necessary?

Many lawyers have not traditionally felt the need to create a matter budget before commencing work on a matter. As Paul Gilbert has noted in his book *Head2Head*, until recently, law firms could "get away with answering the question of 'what will it cost?' with a well-practised sorrowful shrug and a trust-me look".[1]

This approach will rarely wash with clients these days. Even those prepared to pay on the basis of hourly rates increasingly demand to know the likely fee quantum in advance. In this way they can make an informed decision on whether to proceed with a matter, and ensure that they will only be incurring legal fees that they can afford to pay. Again, Paul Gilbert is instructive here when he says, "Can you honestly think of any other purchase decision that is made on the basis of an uncertain outcome, an uncertain price, and an uncertain incidence of when the price has to be paid?"

Certain types of more commoditized legal work have a recognised market price. This might apply to residential conveyancing or drawing up a will. Complex, bespoke transactions do not. Despite solicitors in England and Wales being bound by Code of Conduct requirements, which specify that "you must give your client the best information possible about the likely overall cost of a matter both at the outset and, where appropriate, as the matter progresses,"[2] lawyers have too readily assumed that it is impossible to predict a matter's likely cost when in fact they have often not made any robust attempt to do so.

There is no denying that time and effort is required for a lawyer to produce a reliable cost estimate. Lawyers may have considered that time spent planning a matter was wasted or non-recoverable time. Additionally, the skills required tend not to be taught at law school and as a result, lawyers have felt absolved from the responsibility of accurately predicting a matter's likely cost. This approach is misguided for the following reasons:

- Clients are increasingly refusing to bear all the risk of the cost of a matter and are requiring their firms to offer fixed, capped or value fees. They are also abandoning firms that cannot offer AFAs in favour of firms that can;
- Firms that do offer AFAs must understand what their costs are likely to be or they will not be able to operate AFAs profitably; and
- Firms must understand their costs before agreeing to any rate or fee discounts, or they may find themselves working at a loss, which in the long term becomes unsustainable.

At a minimum, a matter budget will provide the following vital pieces of information:

- The cost to the firm of conducting the matter;
- The fee to be charged to the client; and
- The profit amount and profit margin in percentage terms that will achieved by the firm at the price set.

This chapter will demonstrate how it is possible, even on the most complex matters, to create reasonably accurate matter budgets that will satisfy clients. It will examine the information that a lawyer needs to have available and will provide simple tools which will enable the lawyer to organise and process the relevant data. In turn, this will enable the lawyer to calculate both the cost to the firm and the range of possible fees which could be charged to the client. The actual fee that the firm will finally charge will depend on the strength of the relationship and the ability of the lawyer to negotiate the fee. Advice on fee negotiation is provided in Chapters 7 to 10 of this report.

As a sample transaction, this chapter uses an imagined purchase of shares of a private company in order to illustrate the mechanics of creating a matter budget. Hypothetical UK LLP, the invented law firm introduced in Chapter 4, will act for the purchaser. Accounts for Hypothetical UK LLP were provided in Chapter 4 and further data needed to create the matter budget is supplied in Table 2 of this chapter.

The link between annual and matter budgets

Law firm budgets have become ubiquitous. It would be rare indeed to find a firm these days which had not set a firm-wide budget for the next 12 months, and most likely for a longer period of around three years.

Personal budget targets are also highly pervasive. A majority of firms set billable hours targets for their fee earners. A more enlightened approach sees law firms introducing billing targets which reflect fees earned rather than hours recorded. Lawyers will need to consider their firm and personal targets, and the number of matters that they are likely to complete in the course of a year when setting their prices. If the firm's leadership is transparent with its partners and other fee earners, then they are likely to know the expected profit margin that the firm either aims to achieve as a whole or, more usefully, that the firm leadership expects from their particular practice area.

When pricing a matter, the lawyer needs to be mindful of the profit margin that they are expected to deliver on each matter. There will be occasions when a deviation from expected matter profitability can be acceptable in the interests of securing a new client or developing a new relationship which has a lot of potential. But once a client has become accustomed to working with a law firm at a particular price point, it will be hard to justify raising fees if there is not a commensurate increase in the quality of work or the value provided to the client. In this way, loss leaders all too often translate to losses.

As was emphasised in Chapter 4, there is not much benefit to the firm of fee earners keeping themselves busy with lots of low-margin work (except in volume businesses where this is firm strategy). Personal and firm budgets can guide a lawyer towards the ball park in which fees need to be set if targets are to be met. The amount that the fee earner will be able to charge will of course depend on what the matter is worth to the client and what is considered a reasonable fee for the work to be done. This is the (multi) million dollar question that lawyers struggle with. To answer it, lawyers should deploy historic matter information, matter plans and matter budgets, all of which are explained in this chapter.

Historic price information

While no two matters will be identical, law firms are sitting on a mine of historic matter information, which they would be well advised to take advantage of. They are also constantly generating fresh intelligence to be added to the databank. This information is held both at the individual and institutional level but is not always captured or analysed sufficiently. It is useful both for lawyers to review their own files and for firms to carry out retrospective studies for different, common transaction types.

Some lawyers work on a much higher volume of matters than others and some matters take many months to complete. Many transactions will not complete. This means that there is no right answer as to how many transactions a lawyer should analyse in order to create a credible fee range. There is also no correct response as to how far back in time a lawyer should delve. Much will depend on global and local economic factors as well as the trends in the legal market. In the teeth of a recession, there is little point in looking back at fees charged prior to the downturn. As a rule of thumb, it is probably best to concentrate on the previous two or three years only. This may not produce a wealth of data for an individual lawyer. There will be a much greater volume of data if all similar transactions conducted by the firm or practice group are amalgamated. It will also be very instructive for the lawyer to obtain information about the charging habits of other lawyers in the group. As mentioned in Chapter 4, the large variations between the fees charged by members of a team can often be accounted for by working practices, confidence and negotiation skills, rather than absolute worth of a matter. Practice group heads and individuals can take action to improve their revenue generation in the light of information obtained by a group survey.

As law firm time-recording systems were mainly established for the purposes of generating invoices rather than to support budgeting activity, firms may not be able to obtain the level of granularity that they would like from their firm-wide historic matter information. They should seriously consider the possibility of upgrading their systems for this purpose. In the US, for example, many law firms are now adopting a 'phase and task' approach to time recording, based upon the American Bar Association (ABA)'s billing codes[3] (described further in Chapter 6). Pending firm-wide system development, lawyers can at least use their own memories and examine their own files to provide the nuances – the reasons why one transaction was more expensive than another, which they may not yet be able to derive from firm-wide data.

By looking back over invoices delivered to past clients for similar matters, lawyers can see if patterns and price ranges emerge. Lawyers will need to bear in mind that there are a range of factors which may have influenced the fee that was charged. A list of the key variables which could impact a purchase of a private company is set out below:

- Urgency;
- Value to the client;
- Complexity – for example, multiple jurisdictions, risks within the target or structuring;

- Cooperativeness or hostility of the target, sellers and their advisers;
- Employee issues;
- Regulatory issues;
- Economic conditions affecting the client's ability or willingness to pay and the law firm's need to take on work;
- How the work was won – for example, competitive e-auctions will drive down price;
- The attitude of the client both to working with the law firm and to paying fees;
- The skill and experience of the client;
- The negotiating ability of the lawyer;
- The skill of the lawyer's team assigned to the matter;
- The extent to which the lawyer managed and guided the team;
- Cooperativeness of the client's other advisers – for example, bankers and accountants; and
- Whether the transaction completed or aborted.

Most of these variables will be at play in any corporate transaction. There will be a similar list affecting other transaction types. It is helpful to make a note of any key variables which unduly skewed the final outcome in each transaction.

When pricing a matter, the better the lawyer knows the client and the client's business, the easier it is for the lawyer to predict how easy or difficult the transaction will be and to adjust the price accordingly. If the lawyer has handled similar transactions in the past for the particular client, the lawyer can compare the fees charged to that client with the fees charged for the client group as a whole and make allowances accordingly in the price proposal.

Matter plans

Historic matter information provides the big picture view of the likely overall fee range but this range is still likely to be too wide. Particularly in complex and bespoke matters, the lawyer will need to create a much more detailed matter plan, which shows each anticipated step in the transaction or case and allocates resource and time to completing each step. Not only will the process of creating a matter plan significantly improve the accuracy of any fee estimate, it will also enable the lawyer to estimate the time required to complete the matter; to build the most appropriate team; and, once the matter has progressed, to track performance against plan. The subject of managing a transaction is dealt with in Chapter 6 but suffice to say in this chapter, to manage a matter, a lawyer needs to have some expectations to manage against, whether it is achieving a milestone on time or on budget. If the matter starts to go off track for any reason, the lawyer will be able to make adjustments to the team and their priorities or consult with the client before an overrun becomes an issue.

In order to create a matter budget, the lawyer will need to have considered the tasks to be performed, the skill level required to conduct each task, the available staff and the likely time each task will take. Only by pulling all this information together will the lawyer begin to develop a more accurate picture of the cost to the firm of conducting the matter and the appropriate fee to charge.

Firms should be encouraged to create matter templates for all common transaction types they undertake. If this is not done at firm level, the lawyer can create matter templates for the matter types undertaken by that lawyer. Although data which is more than three years old would need to be treated with great caution in setting a matter price, the tasks required to be undertaken in order to complete any given matter type are likely to have remained static for a much longer period. Therefore, in creating matter templates, lawyers can have recourse to older historic records. A sample matter template for the purchase of a private company is provided in Appendix 1. Alternatively, lawyers may choose to adopt the ABA's Uniform Task-Based Management System referred to above.

The lawyer should create a matter plan for every new matter. The process will be quickest if the lawyer is able to base the matter plan on an existing matter template but the matter plan can be created from scratch if necessary. A summary extract from a matter plan for a purchase of a private company is set out in Table 1. Each major phase of the transaction is described and a number of hours of fee earner time is allocated to each phase. The matter plan specifies how much time should be spent by partners, assistant solicitors and trainees. The information has been condensed here but in reality, each phase should be broken down into its constituent parts as shown in the more detailed matter template in Appendix 1.

The matter plan represents the best guess of the lawyer as to the amount of time that each fee earner will need to spend on each stage of a matter. It is unlikely to be 100 per cent accurate. It can be helpful to create best case and worst case scenario matter plans. The actual amount of time that will be taken is likely to be somewhere between the two.

The best guess will not be wild or uneducated if the lawyer has already followed the advice given above on the use of historic matter information, to provide a realistic basis for the number of hours to be spent. As also mentioned above, the better the lawyer knows the client then the more accurate the matter plan will be. Similarly, the better the lawyer responsible for drawing up the matter plan is acquainted with the deal team and the more they have worked together, the more finely honed the hours estimate will be.

Task	Details	Chargeable hours by fee earner type				Sub total
		Partner	Senior assistant	Junior assistant	Trainee	
1.	Initiating discussions and establishing relationships	10	17	8	0	35
2.	Due diligence	12	15	150	195	372
3.	Structuring	12	15	40		67
4.	Sale documentation	80	240	150	80	550
5.	Completion documentation	4	2	30	8	44
6.	Regulatory advice and clearances	8	40		20	68
7.	Funding arrangements	40	60	60	35	195
8.	Post-completion matters			6	20	26
9.	Co-ordination	35	40	50	25	150
	Totals	**156**	**372**	**436**	**383**	**1,472**

Table 1: Extract from a matter plan for the purchase of a private company

Matter budgets

In order to calculate the fee that can be charged to the client for a matter, the high level outputs of the matter plan need to be fed into a matter budgeting tool. The matter budget is a form of financial model designed to enable lawyers to price their work. At its most basic, the matter budget shows:

- The rates that each fee earner charges;
- The number of hours that each fee earner is expected to work on each of the key tasks to be performed on the matter (with the numbers drawn directly from the matter plan);
- The expected margin that the firm will achieve; and
- Any variance between budget and actual figures.

The lawyer should be encouraged to stress test the model to show what will happen to the profit margin if the number of hours worked is increased while the fee remains static, or if the fee is discounted. It can be quite shocking for a lawyer to see the impact of a ten per cent fee discount on the firm's bottom line.

Table 2 sets out basic information about Hypothetical UK LLP, which will be needed to create a matter budget. Table 3 shows the matter budget for the company acquisition on which Hypothetical UK LLP has been instructed. An explanation of the underlying calculations and a glossary of financial terms is provided in Table 4, while a blank matter budget calculator is set out in Appendix 2. The matter budget can be adjusted by lawyers to meet their needs. If the fee seems too high or the margin too low then the lawyer has the opportunity to adjust the matter plan and matter budget before work on the matter commences. For example, the number of hours of partner time may need to be reduced in favour of more hours undertaken by a senior assistant to deliver the target profit margin. In the short term, if the lawyer realises that the matter cannot reasonably be contained within the fee that the client is prepared to pay, then the lawyer can talk

Hourly rates	
	Standard rate
Partner	£500
Senior assistant	£400
Newly qualified	£200
Trainee	£100

Hours targets	
Partner	1,500
Assistant	1,800
Trainee	1,000

Staff costs			
	Net salary	Tax, social security, pensions	Total salary
Equity partner notional salary	£400,000		£400,000
Senior assistant	£100,000	£25,000	£125,000
Newly qualified	£60,000	£15,000	£75,000
Trainee	£30,000	£7,500	£37,500

Margins			
	Costs per hour (annual total salary/billable hours)	Gross margin per hour on standard rates (standard rate less cost per hour)	Gross % profit margin on standard rates (margin/fee x100)
Equity partner	£267	£233	47%
Senior assistant	£69	£331	83%
Newly qualified	£42	£158	79%
Trainee	£38	£63	63%

Table 2: Hypothetical UK LLP – Budget components

openly with the client about how the matter could be managed differently in order to make it more economic. The client may agree that the timetable can be lengthened, or to take on more of the administrative aspects of managing the matter. The crucial point is that the lawyer is armed with the necessary information before work on a matter commences. And by conducting an informed discussion with the client before any costs have been incurred, the lawyer is likely to arrive at a mutually agreeable position which meets the client's needs yet is affordable and delivers the appropriate profit to the firm.

In the longer term, matter budgets will deliver insights which can inform the firm's business model and strategy. The firm may reach the conclusion that matter processes need a wholesale overhaul in order to be conducted profitably at prices that clients will bear. The firm may need to encourage colleagues to share precedents in order to avoid reinventing the wheel on each matter. And it may become apparent that it is worthwhile or even necessary for the firm to invest in technological solutions, such as automated document assembly, in order to cut costs. The firm may choose to focus its business development efforts on those matters which deliver the greatest level of returns and may decide to withdraw from providing lower margin services. The need to make such decisions is likely to come to light much sooner where firms are forced to consider the profitability of each matter as they create and manage matters to matter budgets. Decisions will be more rational and defensible as a result of being data driven.

A word on tools

The sample matter plans and budgets used in this report have all been created very simply using Microsoft Excel. For lawyers working individually without wider firm support, a spreadsheet is all that is required to create perfectly functional tools. Excel has the advantage of being built into every lawyer's computer and the basics can be mastered very quickly. For these reasons, some firms will choose to roll out firm-wide tools which also rely on Excel.

Other firms will prefer to invest in more specialised technology. There are several off-the-shelf products designed with law firm budget creation in mind, from providers such as LexisNexis, Aderant and Thomson Reuters. However, these tools tend to require a level of user expertise not yet pervasive in law firms. It is likely that such tools will continue to be refined in the coming years. Meanwhile, firms may elect to design software specifically tailored to their needs. Whichever solution is chosen, the firm needs to ensure that its fee earners:

- Appreciate and accept the value to them and to the firm of preparing matter budgets;
- Understand the benefits to them and to the firm of using the tools;
- Are fully trained on the use of the tools; and
- Find the tools simple and intuitive to use.

If these criteria are not met, firms will find that the budgeting tools are neglected and their lawyers continue either to avoid providing fee estimates or regularly underestimate the cost to the firm of conducting a matter, leading to lower than forecast profits or even losses.

This chapter has shown that in an era of increased client activism, few firms can afford to continue to launch directly into working on a matter without first creating a matter budget. In order to create a matter budget, lawyers should bear in mind annual firm and

Hourly statistics					
	Partner	Senior assistant	Junior assistant	Trainee	
Standard rate	£500	£400	£200	£100	
Recovered rate at 80%	£400	£320	£160	£80	
Hourly salary cost	£267	£69	£42	£38	
Margin	£233	£331	£158	£62	

Matter plan					
	Chargeable hours by fee earner type				
Details	Partner	Senior assistant	Junior assistant	Trainee	Subtotal
Initiating discussions and establishing relationships	10	17	8		35
Due diligence	12	15	150	195	372
Structuring	12	15	40		67
Sale documentation	80	240	150	80	550
Completion documentation	4	2	30	8	44
Regulatory advice and clearances	8	40		20	68
Funding arrangements	40	60	60	35	195
Post-completion matters			6	20	26
Co-ordination	35	40	50	25	150
Totals	156	372	436	383	1,472

Matter total fees					
	Partner	Senior assistant	Junior assistant	Trainee	Total
Standard fees	£78,000	£148,000	£87,200	£38,300	£352,300
Recovered fees	£62,400	£119,040	£69,760	£30,640	£281,840
Salary cost	£41,652	£25,668	£18,312	£14,554	£100,186

Matter margins			
	Benchmark	Recovered	Variance
Fees	£352,300	£281,840	£70,460
Salary cost	£100,186	£100,186	
Gross margin	£252,114	£181,654	
Gross margin %	72%	64%	
Other overhead	£114,498	£114,498	
Operating profit	£137,617	£67,157	
Operating profit margin %	39%	24%	51%

Table 3: Hypothetical UK LLP – Simplified matter budget for the purchase of a private company
Adapted from materials provided by Robert Mowbray of Taylor Mowbray LLP, with thanks

personal targets and strategies and should make use of any historic matter information available to them. All this intelligence should be fed into a matter plan which itself will be a component in the matter budget. The matter budget can be used to determine the way that the matter should be resourced, the time it should take to complete and the optimal price to be achieved by the law firm. By manipulating the figures in the matter budget, the lawyer can create a number of pricing options to present to the client in negotiations. The matter budget will also be an essential tool which the lawyer can rely on to manage the matter effectively as discussed in the next chapter. Many lawyers will have had no prior experience of pricing their matters in this way and will need extensive training and coaching to develop their competence and confidence in the new ways of working. Chapter 12 provides more guidance for firm leaders on how to create truly effective learning and development programmes to achieve their goals.

Term	Explanation	Example
Salary costs per hour	Salary cost of the individual divided by that individual's billable hours targets	$\frac{£125000}{1,800 \text{ hours}}$ = £69
Other overhead	Non-salary costs	Usually a separate line item in the profit and loss account
Other overhead percentage	Figure for other overhead divided by turnover and then multiplied by 100	$\frac{£65,000,000}{£200,000,000}$ x100 = 32.5%
Other overhead per matter	Matter revenue at standard hourly rates multiplied by the other overhead percentage	£352,300 x 0.325 = £114,498
Gross margin per hour	The individual's hourly rate less the individual's salary costs per hour	£400 - £69 = £331
Gross margin percentage on hourly rates	Gross margin per hour divided by the hourly rate multiplied by 100	$\frac{£331}{£400}$ x 100 = 83%
Gross margin percentage on overall fee	Gross margin on matter fee divided by matter fee and multiplied by 100	$\frac{£252,114}{£352,300}$ x 100= 72%
Operating profit	Fees less salary costs and other overhead	£352,300 – (£100,186+£114,498) = £137,617
Operating profit margin percentage	Operating profit divided by the fee and then multiplied by 100	$\frac{£137,617}{£352,300}$ x100 = 39%
Net profit	Operating profit plus or minus interest receivable or payable less members' remuneration	(£65,000,000 - £500,000) - £14,500,000 = £40,000,000
Profit per equity partner	Net profit of the firm divided by the number of equity partners	$\frac{£40,000,000}{100}$ =£400,000 per partner
Recovered rate per hour	The standard hourly rate multiplied by the percentage recoverable. So, if a 20 per cent discount is given, the percentage recoverable is 80 per cent.	£400 x 0.8 = £320
Gearing	The number of salaried fee earners for every equity partner, expressed as a ratio	If there are 100 equity partners and 500 salaried fee earners the gearing is 1:5
Lock-up	The time, often expressed in days, between starting work on a matter and getting paid. It comprises work in progress, which is work performed but not yet billed, and debtors which is work billed but not yet paid	If it takes a firm on average 80 days to issue a bill after opening a matter and a further 70 days to get paid then the lock-up will be 80+70 = 150 days

Table 4: A glossary and guide to law firm financial calculations

References

1. All references in this chapter to Paul Gilbert are to *Head2Head*, Paul Gilbert, Author Publishing Ltd, Suffolk, 2002
2. Solicitors Regulation Authority, Solicitors Code of Conduct 2007, Rule 2.03, http://www.sra.org.uk
3. American Bar Association, Uniform Task-Based Management System, http://www.americanbar.org

Chapter 6: Staying within budget – The art of legal project management

"As we know, there are known knowns; there are things we know we know. We also know there are known unknowns; that is to say we know there are some things we do not know. But there are also unknown unknowns – the ones we don't know we don't know." Donald Rumsfeld

THE ESSENTIALS of managing a matter within the budget quoted to a client are:

- Scoping;
- Planning;
- Executing;
- Monitoring and adjusting; and
- Reviewing.

This report has already dealt with scoping and planning. Chapter 5 took a step-by-step walk through the creation of a matter budget. The careful construction of a budget is half the battle in ensuring that a matter can be completed within the estimate or fixed fee quoted to the client. But to ensure success, the budget must not languish disregarded in a file. It must be put to use immediately as the lawyer composes the deal team. The contents of the plan must be communicated to the deal team and the lawyer must refer to it regularly to ensure that the matter remains on track.

The focus of this chapter turns to executing the matter plan, monitoring progress, avoiding scope creep and making adjustments as necessary. This chapter concludes with a thought leadership piece kindly written for this report by Pamela Woldow and Douglas Richardson of Edge International LLC. Their commentary defines legal project management (LPM) and provides an overview of the options available to those looking to implement it within their firms.

Executing the matter plan

Resourcing

The matter plan assigns responsibility for all key tasks within the matter to named individuals. The identity of the person who carries out the work is important for several reasons. First, each individual should take ownership of the area under their responsibility. Professionals such as lawyers generally thrive when they are given ownership and control over what they are doing. Professionals will try to rise to a challenge if they know what they are being tasked with.

Second, any team will be made up of individuals of mixed ability and seniority. This has a number of bearings on the matter. Seniority usually goes hand in hand with increased salary. Deploying more senior personnel will normally imply a higher notional cost per hour to the firm of using that person. Where clients are charged on the basis of hourly rates, the charge to the client for the use of a more senior person is expected to be higher. The reciprocal is that the more senior person can generally be expected to be more knowledgeable and able to complete a task in a shorter amount of time than a more junior person. If the matter plan provides for a person with five years post-qualification experience to draft the contract, but the only person available has three years of experience, the lawyer will need to consider whether adjustments to the matter plan and budget need to be made.

Sometimes partners work consistently with the same team of people whose strengths and weaknesses they know well. Where this is the case, the partner is better able to predict with accuracy the number of hours work that each fee earner will need to accomplish each task. The matter plan is not a theoretical ideal. It is a practical document that needs to reflect reality. It is therefore advisable for the partner to have assembled the matter team before finalising the fee quotation to the client.

Communicating

Communication with both the internal matter team and the client is key to ensuring that the matter plan is adhered to. By sharing the matter plan (or a client-facing version of it) with the client, the partner has the opportunity to validate the plan before work commences. The lawyer and client will be able to discuss openly whether the planned course of action meets the client's needs. If the time scales or the price do not satisfy the client there is a window of opportunity to make adjustments at no cost to the firm.

As mentioned above, it is also vital that the plan is communicated to the deal team. If the partner has allocated ten hours of trainee time to a piece of research but does not tell the trainee, then that individual cannot be blamed for taking 20 hours, half of which will have to be written-off. Communication between the partner and the deal team and the partner and the client needs to continue throughout the course of the matter to ensure that the matter stays on track and any overruns are dealt with accordingly.

Monitoring performance and making adjustments

"As we know, there are known knowns; there are things we know we know. We also know there are known unknowns; that is to say we know there are some things we do not know. But there are also unknown unknowns – the ones we don't know we don't know." The almost mystical words of Donald Rumsfeld[1] encapsulate the vagaries of legal work perfectly.

The course of a matter may not run smooth. Third parties may wilfully obstruct proceedings or events outside any party's control may severely impact the matter plan. A client will not hold the law firm to an initially estimated price (or even fixed fee) provided that the lawyer has agreed the scope of work at the outset of the transaction through the engagement letter and has kept the client informed of any unexpected twists and turns which have transpired during the course of the transaction.

In its 2010 report on the future of fees[2] UK firm CMS Cameron McKenna notes that, "A huge volume of fixed fees are renegotiated at the end of a deal based on scope creep." Such negotiations are always awkward for the lawyer and the client and may prove futile and counter productive to the relationship if the client refuses to accept the validity of the increased fee.

There is a distinction to be made between a firm asking for more money because it did more work than it said it would, and a firm increasing the fee because the client has departed from the original mandate. In the former situation, the client is likely to give the firm very short shrift and will be likely to hold the firm to the original price estimate or fixed fee, unless the firm can demonstrate that the additional work was caused by matters beyond its control, which could not have been reasonably anticipated;

and the law firm communicated effectively with the client at the time that the additional cost was incurred.

In the latter situation, where the client has changed the mandate, the client should be fully prepared to pay the additional fee but the onus will be on the law firm to make it clear to the client at the time that revised instructions are given that these instructions take the matter out of scope.

The client then has the opportunity to consider whether to proceed and will know to expect an increased fee. This is another reason why it is so important for lawyers to create matter plans. Doing so will mean that the scope of work is indelibly in their minds and the lawyer will be aware of any changes to the conduct of the matter, which take it out of scope. If the scope has been shared with the client as it should be, then the client is also more likely to be conscious of when a matter is going off course. Nonetheless, lawyers should not assume that this is obvious to a client. The lawyer may think that there is never a good time to raise the issue with the client but if there is any question of a matter going out of scope then it must be addressed instantly.

This is not just good practice. The Solicitors Regulation Authority new draft Code of Conduct states that clients must receive "the best possible information, both at the time of engagement and when appropriate as their matter progresses, about the likely overall cost of their matter".[3]

Occasionally the law firm will have inadequately scoped the piece of work or underestimated the amount of work involved. This should happen with decreasing frequency as lawyers take the task of scoping work more seriously, become more accustomed to reviewing historic matter data, and practice working with matter templates and matter plans. Some clients will be generous to their firms. Sometimes there genuinely are extenuating circumstances, or the firm may be acting on a truly ground breaking matter and could not have foreseen the amount of work involved.

Generally, however, if firms have agreed to a fixed, capped or value fee, then they can expect to have to take responsibility for not forecasting their costs accurately. After all, they are the experts in the field and have conducted many similar matters in the past – which is why they have been selected. Ultimately the fee earner will have to decide whether to attempt to claw back fees from the client. Again, the earlier in the course of a transaction that a lawyer can give notice to the client that the matter is going out of scope, the more the decision to proceed becomes a joint one and the more likely the client is to accept the cost burden.

The preceding section of this chapter addressed some of the practical day-to-day issues, which present themselves to lawyers at the coal face. In the light of such issues, forward-thinking firms are now looking to introduce a more strategic, planned and managed approach to the matters that they take on. This has spawned the concept of LPM, which is the subject of the final section of this chapter.

Sizing up the legal project management revolution

By Pamela Woldow & Douglas Richardson, Edge International

The emergence of LPM as a worldwide trend continues apace, in scope, form and sophistication. In response to the changing economic imperatives of the legal profession, LPM has taken firm hold in the US and is now crossing oceans to gain traction in diverse legal markets around the world, most notably in the UK, Europe, South America, Australia and the Pacific Rim.

In the US, LPM has emerged from its infancy and begun to mature and move in new directions. Originally used by large US law firms to satisfy major clients' demands for greater predictability, efficiency, and budgetary control, LPM is now morphing into new forms appropriate for smaller firms and a broader variety of clients, while continuing as a powerful tool in high-ticket legal arenas. Already, a number of law schools in the US are building LPM courses into their core curricula. This suggests that it will soon be an essential and accepted part of the fabric of US legal practice.

Equally significant, LPM has become the focus of broadened interest from global firms and others based outside the US. UK-based firm Eversheds led the way in 2008, with its comprehensive project management initiative, which was met with impressive client interest and approval.

Basic LPM constructs appear poised to become the *lingua franca* of the legal profession worldwide, partly in response to client pressures and partly because LPM has established its credibility and potency as it moves into its adolescence.

Because LPM relates to the planning, organisation and measurement of legal activity rather than the substantive content of that activity, its utility transcends national boundaries and legal systems and it will work equally well in civil or common law systems.

Genesis of a trend

The seeds for LPM's growth were sown well before the recent global recession, in large part due to structural changes in law firm size, geographical spread and complexity. However, while the need for better and more businesslike management, control, accountability and performance metrics has been clear for many years, firms (with few exceptions) have resisted changing their service delivery model, which has always allowed firms to pass the costs of doing business through to clients.

The recession changed all that in a hurry. As corporations experienced intense profit squeezes, pressure increased on their legal departments to do the same. This rapidly led to accelerated client demands for better methods to predict, reduce and control the largest component of their budget, outside legal spend. Legal departments' use of convergence programmes, requests for proposals (RFPs), value-based billing and various forms of AFA have increased exponentially, fundamentally altering the power alignment between client and law firm. Clients now have the whip hand, and many are wielding it more aggressively.

Recently these efficiency-promoting techniques have begun trickling down from the domain of big firms serving big clients, to smaller firms feeling increased client pressures for cost effectiveness and predictability. Regardless of size, firms promising these results must deliver on those promises. LPM has become an operational and economic necessity, largely unloved, but the key to maintaining client loyalty and competitive parity.

Defining LPM

American poet Robert Frost once defined freedom as being "when you're easy in your harness". LPM is similar, in that it is basically structured common sense. It is not, as many lawyers fear, a highly complex, quantitatively driven machine, comprised of rigid methods and metrics that allow little room for lawyerly judgment. Unlike industrial project management approaches, such as Six Sigma or Lean, LPM is not intended to create lockstep work processes and invariant critical paths. On the contrary, one of its goals is to provide a flexible framework that enables lawyers of different skills and styles to collaborate more effectively.

There are a variety of approaches to LPM but, however implemented, it offers the following benefits:

- It provides a common vocabulary and infrastructure for all stakeholders;
- It serves as a 'communication engine' to keep all relevant players (both on the client side and the law firm side) fully informed, in agreement and on the same page at all stages of an engagement;
- It provides useful metrics, both to evaluate the progress of an individual engagement and to compare performance longitudinally over a series of projects; and
- It enables law firms to ascertain the actual costs of doing business, which is crucial for planning and measuring profitability in an era where fixed fees will become more common and clients will no longer pay whatever the firm chooses to bill them.

As implemented by law firms, LPM encourages firm, client and task teams to work systematically through a cascade of related steps:

- Collaborating with the client to set project objectives and scope;
- Building a project plan. This includes identifying phases and tasks, identifying project team and stakeholders, building a detailed and realistic budget, creating a communications plan, and anticipating risks, contingencies or unexpected events;
- Executing the plan and using it as a framework for all stages and levels of legal work;
- Measuring progress against the plan, monitoring the budget, and adjusting to changes in project scope or strategy in response to unfolding developments; and
- Post-project review of successes, shortcomings and lessons learned, a process combining input from both the project team and client.

LPM is scalable to the legal matter at hand. Depending on the nature, scope and duration of the engagement (whether a single, simple matter or portfolio of complex, legal matters), LPM can be informal and simple or enormously detailed and complex. The LPM marketplace is expanding at a feverish pitch, with consultants and vendors vying to develop models, methods and tools (LPM-support software programs) that earn recognition as best practices, and capture predominant market share.

Getting started

Implementing LPM is a significant undertaking; one involving some adjustments in the ways lawyers think and behave, but certainly not a fundamental re-engineering of their legal skills and experience. It requires unequivocal commitment from senior firm management and visible support of opinion leaders and 'LPM champions'. There must also be a willing commitment of resources to roll-out an LPM initiative – plan initial implementation, develop useful tools and templates, undertake lawyer and staff training, and establish how to carry initial momentum into long-term LPM acceptance and usage.

Different strategies, different implementation

LPM implementation can be driven by distinctly different strategies and priorities. If a firm's goal is to use LPM as a strong business development lever through rapid deployment, it may elect a horizontal approach – that is, broad-scale immersion into LPM basics that crosses practice lines and disciplines. This approach may involve an intensive series of workshops for lawyers at similar levels (for example, partners and associates) which is often facilitated by outside consultants.

Several years ago, global firm Dechert used this approach to steal the march on its competitors, sparking a rash of catch-up efforts by other large firms and also creating a model for global LPM rollout. Dechert asked partners in all of its US and European offices to attend basic LPM training and, as a true 'first adopter', reaped a huge business development benefit from its efforts. Taking the cue, a major Australian firm contracted well-known US consultants to translate their experience with large US firms into the Australian legal market.

If, on the other hand, the need for LPM grows out of a particular practice area or is responsive to the demands of specific clients, the firm may use a vertical approach to lawyer training, which focuses on the lawyers in a practice group or client team who will be teamed on projects. This approach has three benefits:

- It focuses initial LPM implementation on clients and matters where it will produce the most immediate utility and return on investment;
- It enables the firm to target LPM training to those lawyers and practice groups that already 'have religion' and will commit actively to LPM implementation; and
- It brings together the actual players for hands-on training and lets them practice new skills and techniques together.

As LPM evolves and becomes more broadly accepted, vertical approaches to LPM implementation are becoming more common. For larger firms, the vertical approach phases in LPM more gradually across the firm, easing 'adoption shock'. For smaller firms, it provides an incremental approach to implementation that may require fewer resources than full-immersion roll-outs. A highly successful variant of the vertical approach includes client attendance at training, in order to foster alignment and forge improved communications. Clients universally give rave reviews to this inclusive approach.

Implementing LPM is an exercise in LPM

Firms will not be able to get by simply by going through the motions of implementing LPM as a PR gambit. Clients are more interested in what LPM delivers than in its nomenclature, and they will punish firms that cannot deliver the predictability and control that LPM promises. Lip service is not enough. Perfunctory initial training without follow-up support will not result in anything but superficial LPM name-dropping. The client must see clear and consistent results in terms of accountability and efficiency, in addition to the traditional expectation of legal acumen.

When a firm commits to implementing – or at least exploring – LPM, those responsible for its success will face the need to get a diverse set of interests and stakeholders to collaborate. This includes: firm leadership; practice group and client team leaders; practising lawyers; professional development experts; marketing staff (to capitalise on the business development benefits of proclaiming the firm is LPM-proficient); budget analysts and financial managers; the IT function; AFA committees; possible software vendors or developers; KM experts; and, perhaps, external LPM implementation consultants.

Getting all these players to pull together in harness requires everyone to understand that implementing LPM is an exercise in LPM. That is, the implementation process will require all stakeholders to work through a sequence that includes developing a clear LPM strategy and time frame (both short and long term). This means assembling a multidisciplinary team of committed stakeholders, allocating adequate PTM [people, time and money] resources, developing process and task templates, creating user-friendly budgeting tools, and translating early-stage learning and experience into KM and continuous process improvement.

Of particular importance during the planning process is creating a clear and concise communication plan. Lawyers are not accustomed to such plans, tending to communicate *ad hoc* and in their own idiosyncratic modes. However, poor communication can seriously derail the best-laid LPM plans, so at all stages all players must have a roadmap charting essential stakeholders, appropriate communication pathways, what needs to be communicated and when, and frequency of communication.

Developing essential tools

Firms should never accept the common misconception that LPM is little more than a mindless application of software-driven methods, a kind of automated, 'follow the dots' exercise. Still, effective LPM implementation does require a useful and ever-improving tool kit. This kit includes templates that deconstruct various legal tasks into their constituent action steps, plus tools that aggregate, organise and permit open access to all relevant forms of project information – scope, team, phases and tasks, metrics, communications, and so on. While developing a tool kit does not necessarily require sophisticated software, the best large-scale implementation is supported by accessible, user-friendly templates and dashboards.

LPM is frequently complicated by three barriers:

- Law firms typically do not know what practising law costs, making it impossible to measure actual to budget cost performance;
- Different lawyers do things different ways; and
- Few practice areas have ever sat down to examine the phases and tasks that make up various kinds of engagements.

In order to create practical and complete work process templates, practice groups and clients must take the time to analyse and codify every action every performer undertakes. This sounds more daunting than it is in reality, but it does require a commitment from all players to collaborate to discuss and agree on what steps a certain task or project involves.

In the US, many firms initially build phase and task analysis on the standardised ABA billing codes that have been around for several decades. They may then extrapolate from those codes to meet their practice's unique characteristics or even create entirely new sets of firm-specific codes. Non-US firms, of course, are free to start building their codes from scratch, but the ABA codes remain a useful reference point for them.

Once templates have been developed, LPM implementers may think that much of the heavy lifting is done. However, LPM must explicitly include avenues for evolutionary development: processes and mileposts must be created to review and update templates periodically, in light of lessons learned from post-project review and collective KM.

Predictably, process templates and budgeting tools have improved enormously over the past several years and firms now have a variety of choices among external vendors offering LPM software and solutions that can be integrated into a firm's existing technology platforms.

Many firms initially delegated development of their LPM software support entirely to IT experts, whether internal or outside consultants. This often resulted in fabulously sophisticated tools that many lawyers could not or would not utilise. New generations of tools, which often take the form of dashboards that can be navigated across a variety of project-relevant tabs, have made great strides in user friendliness, speed and the ability to self-populate various fields. Such rapidly-evolving tools do not 'do' LPM, but they certainly support it powerfully.

Overcoming resistance to change

LPM's implications for day-to-day legal practice are potentially so significant that its advocates and implementers can never assume either that it will be embraced by all with open arms, or that its inherent logic and common sense will make an LPM initiative self-executing. Firms entertaining a foray into LPM must expect considerable resistance, especially from senior lawyers who are protective of their positions, prerogatives and compensation.

This resistance means that the implementation team must expect to expend a lot of time and effort securing powerful long-term support from senior management, building buy-in throughout the firm and dealing forthrightly and respectfully with resistance. Implementation efforts also may gain better buy-in if first targeted at practices and practitioners that express a strong need for it. This target cohort should include high-potential future firm leaders and opinion leaders.

The long-term challenge of LPM

The key LPM challenge for any firm is to develop a consistent but flexible LPM approach, which can be used effectively by a variety of lawyers in different practice areas. LPM implementation must eventually extend to all (or mostly all) lawyers and timekeepers, and it must be built into the continuing professional development of present and future generations of home-grown associates, lateral hires and partners in all disciplines.

For LPM to succeed, the firm will have to get its lawyers – who are pressed for time and have revenue generation responsibilities – to collaborate effectively and respectfully with its legal administrator(s) and non-lawyer professionals in HR, IT, finance, and professional development. For all stakeholders, lawyer and non-lawyer alike, the challenge of initiating, implementing and institutionalising LPM will never be a one-and-done deal. It must remain a continuing firm priority, one that will demand continuous improvement as LPM best practices evolve and it becomes the accepted way of doing business throughout the legal profession.

Pamela Woldow is a partner and general counsel at Edge International. She can be contacted at pwoldow@edge-international.com.

Douglas Richardson is a partner at Edge International. He can be contacted at richardson@edge-international.com.

References

1. Donald Rumsfeld, former US Secretary of Defense, US Department of Defense News Briefing, 12th February 2002

2. CMS Cameron McKenna, *The future of fees: your route map to value*, http://www.cms-cmck.com
3. Solicitors Regulation Authority, Draft Code of Conduct, O(1.13), http://www.sra.org.uk

Chapter 7: Overcoming obstacles to negotiating fees

"One of the most common responses from partners when challenged on fees is to give a discount first and worry about the consequences later." Ori Wiener

IT HAS often been observed that lawyers are unafraid to enter negotiations on behalf of their clients and may pride themselves on their negotiating skills, but find it hard to apply these skills when their counterparty is their client. There are many specialist publications which set out the theory and practice of negotiation in detail. Rather than trying to replicate those texts, this report looks at four distinct issues which are particularly relevant to lawyers negotiating fees with their clients.

This chapter examines why lawyers sometimes find it difficult to negotiate with their clients and suggests ways in which they can overcome such obstacles.

Chapter 8 addresses the negotiation process itself. It seems that lawyers do not traditionally prepare themselves for negotiations with their clients, with the same rigour that they would apply to negotiations undertaken on behalf of their clients. As a result, they often find themselves on the back foot during discussions on fees. Chapter 8 will examine the typical negotiation process and will guide lawyers towards wresting control of that process. It will explain, building on the techniques discussed in Chapter 5, how lawyers can prepare themselves for any negotiation.

Chapter 9 answers the question of how lawyers can persuade their clients to pay the desired fee. The emphasis of this chapter is on demonstrating value and creating a range of fee options which are attractive to both the law firm and the client. This is essentially about getting to know each client's needs and then framing fee proposals in ways which respond to those needs.

Chapter 10 moves on to the bargaining and closure phases of a negotiation, which are what people generally think of when they picture a negotiation. It will help lawyers to cultivate the right conditions for a successful negotiation and will provide guidance on how to speak and how to act. The chapter will then move onto a discussion of tactics including how to open the bidding and how to close; before finally surveying some tricks of the trade.

Lawyers face a number of obstacles when it comes to negotiating fees. These obstacles can have such a paralysing effect that the lawyers concerned barely engage in negotiation at all. This chapter examines some of the most common obstacles and suggests ways in which individuals can overcome them. It also provides guidance on how the firm's leadership can ensure that fee earners are well positioned to enter negotiations with their clients.

Overcoming obstacles at the individual lawyer level

Common blocks which inhibit negotiating include:

- Lack of confidence;
- Fear of numbers;
- Ignorance of numbers;
- Embarrassment; and
- Insecure client relationships.

Each of these is examined in turn alongside ways of approaching negotiations which will help individual lawyers.

Lack of confidence

It is very easy for lawyers to succumb to fears that their services will be rejected if their opening bids are too high. However, if bidding starts low, there is no chance of obtaining high prices. Paul Steele and Tom Beasor counsel negotiators not to "be a victim of low ambition".[1] Admittedly, some law firm clients, notably banks, have adopted procurement processes under which they are forced to select only the lowest bidder each time they ask panel members to bid for new assignments. However, this is the exception rather than the norm and few clients select their firms on price alone.

Fear of numbers

A truth ruefully acknowledged by many lawyers is that they entered the legal, rather than the accountancy, profession because they are more comfortable with words than with numbers. Facility with numbers varies hugely across the profession. Some lawyers freeze when asked to discuss figures in real time. Happily there are solutions to this problem. The first is to train and inform lawyers so that they understand their law firm's finances. In particular, to take them through worked examples which show the impact of discounts on profitability as set out in Chapters 4 and 5 of this report.

One-off training has only limited effectiveness. In order to really get comfortable with law firm finance, lawyers who are not naturally numerate will need to have regular refresher courses until the concepts have become second nature. Some lawyers will still feel under-confident. Firms may employ pricing gurus, who spend time sitting down with individual lawyers, helping them to price matters and to work through the possible permutations in advance of a negotiation.

Finally, lawyers should take heart that discussion of the numbers themselves is only a small part of a negotiation. It is just as important to be able to talk about client needs and priorities and how the firm will differentiate itself from the competition by best meeting the client's needs. Lawyers should also be fully conversant with the rationale behind any proposed rates or fixed fee. Again, training, practice, and coaching will make this task much more natural over time, even for those lawyers for whom it was not intuitive at first.

Ignorance of numbers

Fear and ignorance of numbers are allied. Where fear of numbers leads lawyers to avoid discussing fees with their clients, ignorance causes lawyers to agree unprofitable fee structures. Ori Wiener has observed that "one of the most common responses from partners when challenged on fees is to give a discount first and worry about the consequences later".[2] Too often, individual partners do not appreciate the impact that offering discounts to rates or final bills has on profitability. This tends to be the case where partners do not fully grasp law firm economics. As explained in Chapter 4, a discount of 20 per cent may impact a firm's operating profits by over 60 per cent. The exact numbers will vary from firm to firm. The problem is most prevalent in firms which operate a lockstep system of remuneration. In such firms, partners don't immediately feel the impact in their drawings of the discounts that they have personally agreed. Indeed, they may never realise the direct connection between their negotiating behaviour and their income.

Embarrassment

The practice of law is considered by many to be a noble profession and lawyers, through their training and the long-established ethical codes of their regulatory bodies are expected to aspire to the highest professional standards. In some eyes, there is a tension between these exalted principles and the somewhat grubby pursuit of money. Some lawyers are afraid to sully their reputation for professionalism and probity by appearing too money grabbing.

Lawyers' motives to enter the law are very diverse. Some enjoy the intellectual rigour, others want to win recompense for people who have been wronged; to some, the court room appeals as a stage. A lawyer may relish becoming a trusted adviser or may see the practice of law as a training ground for a future career in business or politics. A sizeable number will frankly admit that they are motivated by the prospect of financial reward. Whether or not a lawyer is primarily motivated by financial gain and regardless of the type of work undertaken by a firm, the nature of its clients and the amount of *pro bono* or government funded work it does; legal practices are businesses and must be run for profit. All clients understand this.

Still, some clients cannot afford to pay for legal services, however reasonably priced. Cases of hardship are outside the scope of this report and the decision whether to take such clients on, be it at reduced rates, on a *pro bono* basis or using conditional fees, sits apart from the question of how to budget for and negotiate matters with clients that can pay fees. The fact that firms may choose to act charitably at times does not detract from the central point that law firms are businesses. While clients recognise that they are receiving valuable services from highly skilled professionals who must be remunerated; they do not want to overpay for services. Nor do they want to be taken advantage of, or for costs to spiral with no apparent control. The better a lawyer can justify a proposed price by reference to objective criteria and the value to the client of that service; then the more comfortable the lawyer should feel asking for the fee. Chapter 9 outlines how lawyers can demonstrate their value to their clients and Case study 2 shows how one firm operates value-based billing.

Insecure client relationships

Lawyers dread jeopardising their hard-won client relationships by appearing greedy or by entering acrimonious negotiations. Suppliers of services are tutored in the mantra that 'the customer is always right'. This makes lawyers feel awkward about arguing with their clients. The solution is twofold. Lawyers' pricing must be rational and easy to explain to their clients, in terms which emphasise the value and benefit to the client of engaging the firm at that price. Second, negotiations must not become bad tempered. Once again, the better lawyers understand the rationale behind their pricing and have prepared their negotiating positions (and engaged in constructive dialogue with their clients about needs and priorities) the lower the risk of negotiations degenerating into arguments. There is no place for court room histrionics in negotiations. It is also evident that the more familiar the lawyer is with the client's business and the pressures under which they are operating, and the more frankly that the lawyer can discuss the client's satisfaction with the service provided by the law firm, then the easier it will be for the lawyer to pitch the fee proposal at a level which is likely to meet the client's approval. Such a lawyer can justifiably feel relaxed in broaching the subject of fees in the context of a solid relationship. Ori Wiener's advice to lawyers entering a negotiation is to "be tough on the issues but soft on the people". Handled well, a negotiation can actually enhance a relationship because of the mutual disclosure and sharing which it involves.

Lack of creativity

Lawyers may sometimes jump to the conclusion that they have no scope for negotiating a fee. They may have already sacrificed their entire profit margin and have nowhere lower to go. Alternatively, they may enter a negotiation feeling that the only possible outcome is for them to provide the client with the discount which the client is demanding.

In such circumstances, the lawyer needs to 'think outside the box'. As Fisher and Ury[3] explain in their celebrated book on negotiation, it is a mistake to think that there is only one solution to a problem or that there is only a "fixed pie" to be divided up between the parties. In reality, the lawyer may be able to propose to the client new ways of working together, which provide mutual benefit and which elevate the fee discussions to a whole new plane. This topic is addressed in Chapter 9 which deals with creating options.

Having examined the many measures which individual lawyers can take to help themselves to overcome obstacles to negotiation, the next section looks at ways in which the firm's leadership can enable their lawyers to become better, more fearless negotiators.

Firm-wide support

A law firm's leaders can foster a culture which encourages and supports negotiation by doing the following:

- Providing the right tools;
- Teaching and encouraging;
- Involving business services; and
- Aligning pricing policy and reward mechanisms.

Providing the right tools

This report has already examined the importance of lawyers understanding their firm's economics and preparing well for any negotiation. Firms can play their part in educating fee earners from the newest associates upwards in how to work and behave in ways which promote the economic success of the firm. Over time, such thought processes will become second nature. Chapter 4 outlined the financial information that every fee earner should understand. Rather than forcing them to reinvent the wheel, firms can provide their fee earners with easy to use resources which enable them to prepare budgets and to plan and to project manage their matters.

The appendices to this report contain a number of simple tools which can be adapted by firms. More complex products are available commercially or can be developed by firms themselves. Appendix 1 sets out a *pro forma* matter template for planning the steps in a transaction, allocating responsibilities amongst fee earners and calculating the number of hours work involved in conducting a matter.

Appendix 2 contains a simple spreadsheet, which enables fee earners to forecast the profitability of a matter based on charging a particular fee and the allocation of work amongst fee earners. At the touch of a button, the fee or the number of hours worked or the seniority of the fee earners can be varied and the user of the spreadsheet can view the impact of such variations on profitability. Starting a negotiation with a blank sheet of paper can be daunting and is inefficient.

Appendix 3 sets out a pre-negotiation checklist, which reminds lawyers of the information that they need in order to negotiate effectively and organises that information very succinctly once it has been obtained.

Teaching and encouraging

Having tools is one thing; using them is another. It is depressingly common to hear from partners that their firms do indeed provide budgeting tools but they are not used. The reason tends to be that a brief introductory training session on a new-fangled piece of software is not nearly enough for lawyers to become comfortable with the technology or convinced that the investment of their time in getting up to speed with the tool will be worth their while.

Learning comes about through repetition, familiarity and positive reinforcement. Lessons in budgeting and negotiating need to start early in each lawyer's career and be repeated regularly. Learning by doing is particularly effective. This may start as simulated role plays in training sessions, where young lawyers must think on their feet and act out negotiation scenarios. Before long, they will need to put theory into practice. Newly minted negotiators are likely to be less successful than old hands. Some failure is to be expected. The firm must accept that mistakes will be made. Rather than turning a blind eye, the firm should help the lawyer to recognise the errors made and to learn from them. The firm must ensure that the lawyer does not retreat defeated and afraid to enter negotiations with clients. Successful negotiations should be celebrated and those who have done well should be encouraged to share their knowledge and experience.

Involving business services and experts

Firms employ increasing numbers of individuals in support functions such as KM, business development, IT and finance. However, the relationship between fee earners and members of the support services teams is not always optimised and there is sometimes something of an 'us and them' mentality. In fact, members of the support functions have a great deal to offer fee earners who are struggling with budgeting and negotiating concepts.

Some firms have found that individual lawyers are not ready to prepare budgets and negotiating plans alone. In some cases, these firms have employed pricing gurus or external pricing consultants (or make use of a committee of skilled partners as described in Case study 2). These experts work collaboratively with fee earners. There are even instances of said experts meeting with clients directly and conducting negotiations on behalf of the fee earners. While firms should strive to empower their individual fee earners, the use of such experts can be an enormously positive step for a firm in achieving good pricing outcomes and demonstrating to fee earners what can be achieved and how. Lawyers will become gradually more competent and self-sufficient as they observe the work of the budgeting and negotiating specialists.

Aligning pricing policy and reward mechanisms

It is very important for firms to align pricing policy with their reward mechanisms. It is no use rewarding fee earners for their billable hours if they are being encouraged to negotiate fixed fee deals with their clients. Similarly, consistent cost overruns on fixed price deals cannot be ignored by firms. They must encourage their fee earners to negotiate realistic fees and then project manage their matters to budget. All of the topics discussed in this section are addressed further in Chapter 12.

References

1. All references to Steele and Beasor in this chapter are to *Business Negotiation, A Practical Workbook*, Paul Steele and Tom Beasor, Gower Publishing Limited, Hampshire 1999
2. All references to Wiener in this chapter are to 'Masterclass: Fee Negotiation', Ori Wiener, *Managing Partner*, http://www.mpmagazine.com
3. *Getting to Yes: Negotiating Agreement Without Giving In*, 2nd edition, Roger Fisher and William Ury, Random Century Ltd, London, 1991

Chapter 8: Managing the negotiation process

"A process through which parties move from their initially divergent positions to a point where agreement may be reached." Paul Steele and Tom Beasor

LAWYERS WHO avoid thinking about and discussing fees with their clients are likely to be hijacked by unexpected demands from their clients to discount their rates or overall fees. The conversations are likely to come up at inconvenient times when lawyers do not have the relevant numbers and arguments readily available to back-up their rates or fees.

When negotiations start on the back foot

'You said how much?'
'You must be joking.'
'We're not going to pay that.'
'But you said you could do it for £50,000.'
'We've only got approval for the amount you estimated.'
'Remind me, why are we paying for your trainees?'

Rather than wait for this to happen, lawyers should take control of the negotiation process. It is worth remembering that the balance of power in a fee negotiation (the law firm's leverage) shifts over time. During the law firm selection process, the client has a strong bargaining position but the firm also has the opportunity to differentiate itself through its willingness to engage with the client on fees and to work collaboratively to achieve fee structures that both parties will be happy with. The law firm's leverage will be greatest when it has been appointed (subject to agreement on fees) but work on the matter has not yet commenced. Once a matter is under way, although the client is relatively unlikely to change firms part way through the process, the firm's negotiating leverage will gradually decrease as it sinks more cost into the matter. At the end of the matter, the client's position is once again strong and, if the client objects to the bill, very few firms will sue their clients for payment. Lawyers who continue to rack up fees throughout a matter, without due consultation with their client, will almost certainly find themselves in very uncomfortable negotiations about fees after the time has been incurred. It is far better to consider the matter up front and throughout the course of the transaction, and address any unexpected overspends – preferably before they arise. In this way, the client can approve the additional costs, or the client and the firm can change tactics to reduce spend before time on the clock is incurred, which may be irrecoverable.

Negotiation stages

Paul Steele and Tom Beasor have described negotiation as "a process through which parties move from their initially divergent positions to a point where agreement may be reached".[1] In other words, negotiation is a process. Parties are expected to start out with different interests and goals but if the negotiation is successful, they reach a mutually satisfying position. This is a more constructive view (particularly in a law firm context, where it is hoped that the parties will have an ongoing relationship) than to characterise a negotiation as a fight with winners and losers.

Negotiations may take place *via* a series of meetings, phone calls, exchange of correspondence or a combination of different methods. Regardless of the number of negotiating sessions, there are four distinct phases of every negotiation. These have been neatly categorised by Nic Peeling[2] as:

- Preparation;
- Sharing;
- Bargaining; and
- Closure.

It is easy to focus only on the bargaining stage of a negotiation. The next few pages explain why this would be short-sighted and provide a step-by-step guide through the preparation and sharing phases of a negotiation. Bargaining and closure will be dealt with in Chapter 10.

Preparation

The importance of this stage cannot be over emphasised. To prepare for a negotiation, a lawyer must think through his or her position and marshal all the information that can be mustered to help the lawyer to understand the client's likely objectives, sticking points and position.

The context

Preparation should not be restricted to calculating the fee that the firm would like to achieve, although this is important. The starting point is to consider the context in which the negotiation will take place. For example, in a set-piece negotiation, who will be involved from each side and what will their roles be? Which person from each party has the authority to sign-off any deal? Understanding the sales cycle is also vitally important. Different approaches will be required depending on whether the lawyer is persuading the client to engage the firm or whether the engagement is secure but only the price remains undecided. The negotiating stance will be influenced by the sort of relationship that the firm hopes to obtain with the client. Is the lawyer trying to secure a one-off piece of work or looking forward to securing a long-term relationship, perhaps across the whole firm? Critically, the lawyer should always be thinking about what matters to the client and what the client will be like to work with. This will become more apparent during the 'sharing phase' of the negotiation but the lawyer should gather together any available intelligence in advance of entering negotiations in order to prepare a number of pre-planned negotiating positions.

Ensuring profitability

The lawyer needs to have calculated the fees or rates that they would like to charge in advance of entering a negotiation. The tools and skills on budgeting described in Chapter 5, and the templates provided in Appendices 1, 2 and 3, can be used for this purpose. By altering variables such as the number and seniority of fee earners, hours worked and the scope of the engagement, the lawyer will be able to come up with a range of prices which will meet the firm's profitability criteria. They will also know when a fee offered by a client is unacceptably low. Chapter 9 deals with optimising the fee and demonstrating value to the client.

Pricing competitively

Identifying the firm's competitors and how they price (where possible) can helpthe lawyer to start pricing discussions in the right ball park. Reliable competitive information is hard to come by in the legal sector. Lawyers are rightly wary of sharing information outright for fear of allegations of collusion and fee information may be considered confidential by firms. With the exception of those carrying out commoditized work, firms seldom charge (or realise) their full rate card. The deviations from standard rates are so diverse and the matters themselves are so often considered unique that lawyers may not have any meaningful comparators to work from. Some benchmarking data is available commercially. For example, PricewaterhouseCoopers (PwC) produces an annual survey of billing rates. This shows not only selected law firm's standard rates, but also the ones that they agree with clients (worked rate) and the rates eventually billed (effective rate). Separate surveys are produced for the US and the UK.[3] Such information on rates can be useful but does not tell the lawyer what the overall fee would have been on particular types of transaction.

A relatively new product has been launched by CT Tymetrix, which claims to be the "first and only of its kind" in providing a "guide to the pricing of services throughout the legal industry".[4] This may prove to be a useful reference point for some firms.

Lawyers should be encouraged to draw on their own firm's historic billing information to build a range of prices which have, at least historically, been seen as acceptable to some clients for each matter type. Even this information may be tricky to obtain as firms may not have coded their time recording information in a useful, task-based manner. Lawyers may have to fall back on personal historic billing patterns as a guide. All historic information needs to be treated with caution as economic forces, technological innovations and new market entrants may have impacted the prices that clients are willing to pay.

Strategy

Before entering the negotiation, the lawyer or firm will need to decide the extent to which they are prepared to move from standard rates or the opening price. If the firm is not willing to move at all then there is in fact no negotiation – but there may be no agreement either. So, the firm may find itself losing clients as a result of taking too rigid an approach. Whether attending a meeting alone or with a wider team it pays to have thought through the opening position, some affordable concessions (not restricted to price alone) and critically, the walk-away point. More advice on determining the walk-away point is provided in Chapter 10.

Roles

Many negotiations between lawyers and their clients take place simply between one client and one lawyer, generally a partner. However, in larger tender exercises there may be a number of participants from both sides at negotiation meetings. If fielding a team, the law firm must decide who will be the lead negotiator. This may not be as obvious as it sounds but experienced negotiators with proven track records tend to get better results than technical subject experts, whose skills lie more in the execution of the work. The lead negotiator will need to control the other members of the team. This is more easily done if all offers are channelled through that individual. It is useful for the team to pre-agree a non-verbal signal for 'stop talking now'. If the numbers are really complicated it may be helpful to field the firm's finance director or pricing czar (if such a person exists) to deal with the financial implications of the offers on the table. Many firms now employ account managers for their most important clients. If they have developed really strong relationships with the client, particularly the decision maker, then their presence can be useful. However, large teams are unwieldy and meetings become less intimate. In Case study 3, a legal procurement manager provides a personal perspective on effective law firm negotiation teams and techniques.

Although most obviously relevant to planned negotiations, most of the advice set out above is applicable to *ad hoc*, informal negotiations. Even if a client rings unexpectedly to request a discount or rebate, the lawyer should still go through many of the routines outlined above. The initial conversation can be used to understand what the client is asking for and why. The lawyer will then need to carry out a price analysis, before commencing the bargaining and finally reaching closure, all as outlined above. Although sometimes panicked into doing so, lawyers should not be required to conduct the whole negotiation from start to finish during the initial call, and most clients would understand a lawyer's need to reach a considered position and to obtain necessary approvals.

A client initiating a surprise call about pricing may expect to come away from the discussion in a better position than the other person, because they have had the advantage of preparation. To help level the playing field, when opening a new client matter, lawyers could use the simple pre-negotiation checklist provided in Appendix 3 of this report. In this way, the lawyer would embark on any price discussion from a strong and well-informed position.

Sharing

Any negotiation meeting, however formal, should commence with a conversation during which the parties exchange important background information and set the ground rules for their negotiation. In addition to the words that are spoken, this is the time in which relationships are built and as such, this phase can strongly influence the tenor of the negotiations.

During early conversations, both parties should try to steer clear of financial matters and instead bring their non-financial concerns into the open. A client may want assurance that the lawyer (or firm) will be able to field a consistent team, work under pressure, have sufficient gravitas to speak directly to the board of directors, and so forth.

This early and hopefully non-combative phase of discussions can also be used to clarify each party's expectations for the outcome of the meeting and how it will be documented, as well as any time constraints.

Each party may casually drop certain observations into the conversation, which are calculated to influence the other party's negotiating behaviour. For example, if a lawyer says 'I'm incredibly busy right now, we're seeing a huge surge in rights offerings this quarter', the client will understand that the law firm is not desperate for work. Some law firms will pride themselves on offering a premium service, which commands premium rates. By making this clear, the conversation can be steered onto the premium nature of the service and the client will know in advance that this firm will not be the cheapest in the market, and will adjust its expectations accordingly. The negotiation may then focus on matters other than price, such as speed of delivery or quality of work, which the law firm may be more comfortable discussing.

Sometimes the parties will decide to put deal breakers and walk-away scenarios on the table at the outset. They will do this if they feel that they are either so important that they must be brought to the fore or because they think that this will give them power during the negotiation. A client might say 'I'm only willing to appoint your firm if you agree to provide all of your work on the basis of fixed fees. Can you agree to that or shall I look elsewhere?' This is a risky strategy, which can backfire and so lawyers should think carefully before employing it themselves.

The meat of the discussion between the parties should consist of the client explaining their requirements to the lawyer and the lawyer asking probing, interested and intelligent follow-up questions. This will enable the lawyer to craft a proposal which fulfils the client's needs and demonstrates value. Chapter 9 explains how lawyers can demonstrate value, while Chapter 10 provides more detail on how to ask the right questions in a negotiating meeting.

Bargaining and closure

Having set ground rules and expectations, the bargaining phase is where fees are discussed. Closure, as its name suggests, is the final part of a negotiation where discussions reach a conclusion and agreement is recorded. Both of these phases are discussed extensively in Chapter 10.

References

1. All references to Steele and Beasor in this chapter are to *Business Negotiation, A Practical Workbook*, Paul Steele and Tom Beasor, Gower Publishing Limited, Hampshire 1999
2. *Brilliant Negotiations*, Nic Peeling, Pearson Education Limited, Harlow, 2011
3. The PricewaterhouseCoopers Billing Rate & Associate Salary Surveyplus
4. http://www.realratereport.com

Chapter 9: How to obtain the desired fees and structures

"Price is what you pay; value is what you get." Warren Buffett

Distinguishing value from price

Warren Buffett, the renowned investor and industrialist, has written that "price is what you pay; value is what you get".[1] Lawyers' fees, at least at the high end of the market, are priced on a matter by matter or client by client basis. Hourly billing (or cost plus billing as it is sometimes known) enables a firm to charge for its effort. Most clients are uninterested in how hard a firm has to work. Instead, clients concentrate on the value or utility of the services that they will receive. A firm will need to know how many hours it will have to expend on performing a matter in order to establish how much it will cost the firm to provide the service to the client. That is why the number of hours to be worked is a central feature of a firm's matter plan and budget, regardless of whether it is charging on the basis of hourly rates or offering AFAs. The price to be charged to the client needs to exceed the cost to the firm of carrying out the work but that will not be the determinant of value for the client.

Ronald Baker, an expert in pricing for professional services firms, says that only a minority of clients are totally fixated on price. He explains that "people are not just price sensitive; they are value conscious".[2] In order to secure an engagement and agree a fee or hourly rate, a law firm first needs to impress its value proposition upon the client. The firm must persuade the client that it is 'worth it'.

Baker notes that some professionals have become so wedded to the concept of charging based on the number of hours worked that they feel that it is somehow morally wrong to charge a fee which is substantially in excess of the cost to the firm of conducting the matter, plus the firm's standard profit margin. Baker dismisses this philosophy as being simply as case of "poor self-esteem". He advises professional services providers to aim to achieve super profits through value pricing. Value in this context does not mean 'cheap'. Taking an economist's view of value, Baker describes a value fee as "the maximum amount that a given customer is willing to pay for a particular service, before the work begins". It should be noted that value is determined on a client by client basis and that it must be established and agreed with the client before substantive work on the matter commences. Value may be perceived differently after a matter has been completed. Regardless of the benefit which the client has received, the law firm's bargaining power will be very much reduced after the services have been rendered.

Determining value

Having shown the importance and benefits to a firm of charging for value, the next section of this chapter has been written to help law firms to demonstrate value to their clients.

Providing valuable services

Firms quite often talk in general terms about the value that they offer to their clients. There isn't a large commercial firm in existence which doesn't claim to have 'deep sector knowledge' and to 'understand our clients' businesses'. Most firms state that they offer 'commercially focused advice' and that they are 'relationship driven'. A firm that did not do this would not be in business for long. However, such generic descriptions of value do little to differentiate one firm from another and, most importantly, do not address the question of how the law firm will meet a particular client's personal expectations of value.

Firms do not find it easy to enunciate the value that they provide to individual clients but this skill is absolutely central to justifying the firm's charges and is ignored by firms at their peril. The reason that value seems so ephemeral is that it is totally subjective. Firms must be able to capture and convey to their clients the value that they provide in terms that are meaningful to each client.

The only way law firms can establish value is to engage with their clients. However, few clients can provide a straight answer to the seemingly straightforward question, 'what does value mean to you?' The law firm is likely to have to tease out the answer by asking pertinent questions. One head of pricing likes to ask "What is your pain?" The answers will enable the client to formulate appropriate pricing solutions. Some common issues and how the firm might deal with them are set out in Table 1.

In determining the value of its services to a client, the law firm should also consider the following factors.

Substitutability

How easily the client could obtain similar services of an equivalent quality from the firm's competitors or whether the firm is able to provide anything unique, in terms of technical expertise, geographical reach or knowledge of the client.

Relative cost

Perceptions of value may be linked to how significant the expenditure is for the client. In other words, the relative cost of the service, rather than simply its absolute cost.

Significance of the matter

An equally salient factor is the importance of the matter to the client. It is well known that clients are much less price sensitive on 'bet the company' matters than on more routine transactions. Although both the absolute and the relative expense for the client may

Client's 'pain'	Value creation
Monthly cash flow constraint but indifferent to total cost	Offering monthly, capped payments, spread over a period of time.
Pressure of work	■ Taking on work burden; ■ Operating a simple billing process which requires minimal client effort; ■ Acting autonomously on the client matter; and ■ Preparing high-level briefings rather than detailed memoranda.
Unhappy with previous firm	■ Emphasising the quality of the firm's service offering; ■ Providing testimonials and access to referees; and ■ Explaining how previous areas of discontent will be addressed.

Table 1: Pricing for the client

be high, the impact of failure may be so significant as to justify very high legal fees.

Matter outcomes
The law firm would be well advised to think about the client's goals in instructing the firm. For example, a real estate lawyer may think that the firm has been instructed simply to draft the lease of an office building. For the client, securing the lease may mean that staff who have been scattered across several run-down offices in sub-prime locations will be united in one convenient building, which will be fitted out to suit the client's requirements. Staff morale and productivity may increase as will co-operation between teams, and total rental expenditure may decrease. The client will therefore expect that the timely completion of the lease will reduce staff attrition and increase profitability. The law firm will better encapsulate the value which will be provided by executing the lease speedily, if it can couch the description of the service that it will provide in these client-centric terms.

Providing value-added services

When firms are asked to describe the value that they provide to their clients, they sometimes point out the raft of value-added services that they make available to their clients. These take many forms, which can be broken down into categories such as provision of knowledge, access to resources, IT solutions, and client relationship management (CRM) tools. A list of typical value-added services offered by large law firms in the UK is shown in Table 2. There is considerable overlap between the categories. For example, an intranet is an IT tool, which fosters CRM, makes it easy to share information, and provides know-how.

Value-added services are often provided free of charge to the client as they are seen as non-core overlays to the firm's traditional advisory and transactional work. Firms do sometimes charge for some of these services, or may charge some clients but not others. An example is the Blue Flag service (described in Chapter 3) which is available from Linklaters on a subscription basis.

Certain services such as newsletters and training have become ubiquitous. Clients receive many competing offers from their firms and may take some for granted. However, they would most certainly miss them if they were not provided. Clients consider some value-added services to be critically important to their businesses or their legal departments. For example, some would find it hard to function without the secondees that they receive, or the training services and free helplines that their firms provide.

When it comes to tendering for business, clients pay considerable attention to the value-added services that firms provide and firms can cite such services as differentiating factors. Firms recognise this and put

Knowledge	Resources	IT solutions	CRM tools
Training Newsletters Personalised alerts Standard documents Research	Library and computer facilities Use of databases and subscription services Helplines Meeting space Provision of secondees	Intranets Deal rooms Contracts databases Know-how Standard documents Templates Tool kits	Intranets Billing services Client feedback programmes

Table 2: Value-added services

considerable effort into developing their offerings, which are necessary but by no means exhaustive ways of demonstrating value to their clients.

Creating options

Law firms are sometimes under the impression that they need to issue the client with a single price proposal, which is then likely to be negotiated down. In fact, when clients ask for creative pricing proposals, they are often pleased to be presented with a number of options. The client will choose the option which provides the best value in accordance with their current needs.

Ronald Baker advises firms to present three pricing options. He cites research which shows that firms will "nudge clients up the value curve" if they offer three options rather than two. In other words, firms will sell more services at higher prices if they each offer expensive, mid-range and cheap options. Clients will tend to pick more services in the middle range and fewer from the bottom, which they will treat with suspicion.

There are two main levers which firms can employ in creating pricing options. They can either find ways to reduce the cost to the firm of performing the service, or improve the benefit to the firm of selling the service. Whichever route is chosen, the firm should ensure that it achieves or exceeds its target profit margins. Examples of how this can be done are set out below.

Reduce cost to the firm

A large national firm may have a number of regional offices which have a lower cost base than the London office. The client may be happy to receive services from regionally based lawyers in order to save cost. Alternatively, the client may be willing to take on some of the administrative burden of running a project, so that fees are directed towards paying for expert legal advice rather than administrative services, which can be obtained more cheaply elsewhere.

Increase benefit to the firm

If a firm can obtain an annual retainer or an exclusive mandate for a substantial portfolio of work, this will be more beneficial than merely securing a place on a client's panel – as a panel place only confers the right to bid for individual matters on a piecemeal basis. Taking the example of a firm being instructed by a human resources department on an unfair dismissal claim; the firm might offer a fee of £15,000 to handle the claim.

Alternatively, the firm might propose a fee of £13,500 for each single plaintiff employee claim over the course of the next 12 months, in exchange for the exclusive right to handle the employee litigation portfolio. There are a number of possible permutations depending on the size of the client's litigation portfolio, the complexity of the cases, the historic charges that the firm has levied when working on the basis of hourly rates, and the proportion of cases which settle out of court.

In all cases, the client obtains greater predictability of spend and the firm knows in advance the budget it must work within. The firm also has certainty of income, improved cash flow and, therefore, lower financing costs. The fees should be calculated to ensure that the benefits of repeat work and improved cash flow offset the apparent discount, in order to maintain or even increase profitability.

The firm can either openly present pricing options to the client and then discuss which option is the most attractive. Or it can present an initial proposal but hold the other options in reserve. In this way, the firm may appear to be ready to make concessions to meet the client's requirements. But in fact, each of the options has been worked out in advance and is calculated to be attractive to the law firm.

Ingredients of winning proposals

In summary, in order to obtain the fees that it desires, the law firm needs to:

- Recognise the difference between price and value;
- Establish what value means for each client at any given point in time; and
- Prepare a range of alternative fee structures which will deliver the financial returns sought by the firm.

Appendix 3 contains a pre-negotiation checklist, which has been designed to prompt lawyers to perform these steps each time they are invited to pitch for, or take instructions on, a new client or a new matter.

References

1. Warren Buffett, writing in a letter to the shareholders of Berkshire Hathaway Inc., 2008. In the letter, Buffett ascribes the concept to Ben Graham, an American economist and proponent of value investing. Also quoted by Baker (see below).
2. All references in this chapter to Ronald Baker are to *Implementing Value Pricing: A Radical Business Model for Professional Firms*, Ronald Baker, John Wiley & Sons, Inc., New Jersey, 2011

Chapter 10: Tips, tactics and tricks

"There is never a good sale… unless it's a good buy for the customer." Stanley Marcus

THIS CHAPTER focuses on the final two stages of a negotiation: bargaining and closure. It is divided into three sections. The first, on tips, provides guidance on how best to behave in a negotiation – in particular, how to speak, listen and act. The second, on tactics, covers approaches to bidding, making concessions and closing. The final section deals with tricks, which are addressed from three angles. The section begins with 'tricks to embrace', which are really tools of the trade, rather than any kind of underhand ploys. The second category of tricks are those which can be employed, but with caution. They are perfectly ethical but can be counterproductive. The last set of tricks cross the ethical line and are not recommended. Quite apart from the requirements of professional ethics, behaving with integrity is fundamental to building relationships. Not all counterparts will behave fairly and occasionally, lawyers may be on the receiving end of the kind of less palatable behaviour which is exposed in this section. Forewarned is forearmed.

Tips

Making everyone a winner

A win-win negotiation is one which achieves a pleasing outcome for both the law firm and the client. Lawyers would be well advised to adopt the maxim of Stanley Marcus, former chairman of the luxury retailer Neiman Marcus, who learned from his father (the founder of the store) that "there is never a good sale… unless it's a good buy for the customer".[1] The secret of success is to ensure that the client feels that they have obtained a pleasing result. This does not mean that the lawyer has to accede to all the client's requests. It is about perception. Even if the lawyer is secretly delighted with the result achieved, it is important that the client should believe that they have obtained some important concessions. How to make concessions and easy trades is dealt with later in this section. Most importantly, as described in Chapter 9, the deal struck must represent good value in that particular client's eyes.

Using leverage

It is easy to be overawed by the market power of a big name client and lawyers may assume that the client's size will enable them to dictate terms. However, law firms in such circumstances need to be aware of their own worth. A niche law firm – for example, one supplying specialised telecoms advice to a large corporate – may be in a powerful position if there are few firms with similar expertise.

Leverage is also a question of timing. A law firm's leverage in a fee negotiation is strongest when the client has selected the firm as being the most capable and desirable to carry out the work, but before the work has begun. By contrast, firms which only enter fee negotiations after a matter has been completed and an invoice rendered will be seriously disadvantaged. In the words of Ronald Baker, "a service needed is always worth more than a service delivered".[2]

Deploying the experts

With practice, everyone can radically improve their negotiation skills. However, negotiation will come more easily to some people than others. Firms can organise themselves so that those with the greatest skill at winning business spend a greater proportion of their time winning business for the firm. In other situations, it may be a case of identifying who has the best relationship with the client. If a member of the firm knows the existing or potential client well, be it through past engagements or through social interaction, it may make sense to field that person. Some lawyers will be afraid that the negotiation will jeopardise their relationship with the client, but this should not be the case if the lawyer takes a relationship based, win-win approach to negotiation, as advocated in this report.

Active listening

Lawyers negotiating with clients should make sure that they are mainly listening rather than talking. David Maister has said that "professionals talk too much". Putting himself in the shoes of a client, he continues, "If I'm talking, telling you about my company and my needs, you're ahead; if you're talking, you're losing."[3]

Asking questions

In addition to their vital importance in ascertaining the client's wishes, questions are very powerful tools in their own right. So much so, that Ian Cooper has written a book entitled *Just Ask the Right Questions to Get What You Want.*[4] In it, Cooper explains that questions can be used to great effect in a number of ways. As a general premise, he suggests that asking questions is much more effective than making statements. Cooper provides ways in which questions can be used in negotiations. Some of these suggestions, which have been tailored for use by lawyers, are set out here.

- An awkward question, one that the lawyer isn't able, or ready, to answer can be parried with a further question. For example, when asked 'what will you charge for this matter?', a lawyer might answer 'what would you be prepared to pay?'
- The lawyer can ask questions in order to find out more about the client's priorities before naming a price. Again, in response to the same question above, the lawyer might say 'what is your timetable for this matter; is it urgent?' The answer can help the lawyer to determine how the matter would need to be staffed, its importance to the client and whether speed is more valuable than price. All of this information will have a bearing on the price that the lawyer can charge.
- Questions can be used to direct a client's thinking. Rather than saying, 'would you like to work with us?', the lawyer could say 'when would you like us to start work?'
- Another way to direct a client to a favourable position, is for the law firm to present the client with choices that would all be advantageous (or at least satisfactory) to the firm. For example, if asked, 'Would you rather X or Y?', the client is more likely to elect one of the options, rather than insisting on Z.

Building rapport

As one law firm veteran said, "lawyers will do anything to avoid talking to clients about fees". This is not just because lawyers may be outside their comfort zone discussing numbers. They may also fear that the conversation immediately places them in an adversarial position, in relation to their clients. This does not have to be the case. The lawyer should concentrate on creating a warm and collaborative tone, a feeling of being in it together, looking for solutions that will be fair to both sides and will build a successful working partnership. This should not be confused with taking the client's side. As Nic Peeling writes, "empathise, don't sympathise".[5] Empathy will enable a lawyer to understand and predict a client's behaviour but sympathising leads to concessions.

Before even considering mentioning the fee, the lawyer should try to develop a rapport with the client. This will happen naturally if the lawyer has begun the discussion by displaying interest in the client by using appropriate questions. Finding some areas of common ground helps. These could be on a work or personal subject, although people vary enormously in the degree of personal disclosure that they are comfortable with giving or receiving. The aim is to be friendly but with the intention of cementing a business relationship, rather than making friends.

It is usually easier to build rapport during a face-to-face meeting than over the telephone or by email. This is particularly true if the parties have never met before. Although a face-to-face meeting can be more daunting (there is nowhere to hide) it is generally worthwhile.

Creating the right expectations

The lead-up to naming the fee can help to condition the client to find that price acceptable. For example, if the lawyer lets it be known that they are very sought after, the client will understand that the lawyer can be picky over the assignments taken. If the lawyer knows that there are cheaper operators in the market, they can acknowledge that their firm is not the cheapest, but reaffirm that the service is of a very high quality and, as such, represents the best overall value.

Focusing on interests, not positions

In their seminal book on negotiation, *Getting to Yes*,[6] Roger Fisher and William Ury emphasise the importance of focusing on interests rather than positions. It is all too easy to take a position such as 'we won't reduce our hourly rate below £350' and become stuck there. Whereas it is better to think about what each party wants to achieve, which in the law firm's case may be an operating profit of 30 per cent. Or in the client's case, it might be a total spend of no more than £10,000. By using different fee earners or changing the scope of work it should be possible for both parties' interests to be met.

Focusing on problems not people

Fisher and Ury again stress that although "negotiators are people", the negotiation should be about the issues that are on the table and how they can be solved. It should not be about personal point scoring or emotional behaviour.

Correcting errors

If the client has misunderstood or a mistake has been made, it should be corrected immediately. Admit to a mistake if necessary. It is much better to deal with it when it is fresh, than to try to go back at a later date.

Using appropriate language

Conversations in a business setting should not be over familiar, but neither should they be so formal that they are stilted. The degree of formality will depend on how well the parties know each other, the number of attendees and the meeting purpose. Behavioural norms vary considerably from country to country and there can even be quite marked behavioural differences between business sectors. Books that attempt to convey the appropriate language, approach and style to be adopted when dealing with different cultures are available, but there is no substitute for local experience. If in doubt when negotiating abroad or with people from other countries, it can be helpful to observe and adapt to the way that the other side behaves. This can work well provided it does not cross the line into mimicry.

Observing body language

Most communication is non-verbal. Experts estimate that as much as 93 per cent of communication is through body language and only seven per cent is based on the words that we use.[7] Lawyers should be aware of the non-verbal signals that they send to their clients. By reading their client's body language, lawyers will be able to sense their attitudes, moods and reactions to the proposals on offer. Numerous books have been written on the subject of body language. A short primer (drawing on the *eBusiness Master Guide to Body Language Basics*) is set out below to guide lawyers embarking on negotiations.

The opening

A meeting will often start with a handshake. This creates the first impression. A firm but not an iron grip should be used. The aim is not to crush the 'opposition'. In most cultures, a smile goes a long way.

Creating atmosphere

Sitting back comfortably signals that the person is relaxed, confident and engaged. Perching anxiously on the edge of the seat reveals nervousness but slouching also gives a poor impression.

Faux pas

There are a few habits and ticks which are best avoided over the negotiating table.

- Crossing arms – appears hostile or defensive;
- Yawning, drumming fingers, tapping feet and sighing – all signs of boredom; and
- Chewing fingernails and other turn-offs.

Reading the client

A range of emotions are commonly experienced at various points during negotiations. The most frequently encountered emotions and the gestures which often accompany them are summarised here:

- *Engaged, listening and thinking* – smiling, looking up, palms facing up and soft eye contact are all encouraging signs.
- *Defensive, disagreeing or angry* – arms crossed, hands in pockets or on hips, clenched fists, thumping the table, rubbing or pinching nose, wrinkled nose, pursed or biting lips or raised voice. If the client is thumping the table or shouting and spluttering with anger then their feelings should be fairly obvious.
- *Bored* – arms crossed, hands in pockets or on hips, pacing, looking at the time, glancing around, yawning, sighing, tapping fingers or feet. Several of these behaviours at the same time and the meeting really needs to draw to a close.
- *Shame* – rubbing nose, a false smile (lips only, no warmth from the eyes), losing eye contact (person is ashamed), sudden crossing of arms or legs (defensive

or hostile posture). If any of these behaviours are exhibited then the client's words may not truly reflect their thoughts.

Room for misinterpretation

Interpreting body language is not an exact science. One action may be susceptible to a number of interpretations. Sometimes a person changes their body language for physical reasons unconnected to their emotions. Crossing the arms is typically seen as hostile but it is also a common reaction to feeling cold. Pinching the nose could signal anger, but perhaps the person is restraining a sneeze. The best advice is not to rely on one data point alone but to keep all senses alert and to try to be sensitive to the reactions of the client. Finally, a word of warning for those engaged in cross-border transactions. Body language does vary across geographies. Most confusingly, nodding the head may mean 'yes' in one country and 'no' in another. For those lawyers about to embark on significant negotiations with people from other cultures, it can be worth checking such potential pitfalls in advance.

Remembering that is not all about money

Negotiations aren't all about money. They may be about service levels or speed. They also provide opportunities to learn about the client and to enhance the relationship. This should be the starting point of any negotiation and the information gleaned should be used throughout the process. During the course of a negotiation, the client may reveal valuable information about competitors' service levels, strengths, weaknesses and pricing. This intelligence can be used in the current negotiation and in subsequent interactions with clients.

Tactics

Opening gambits

A perennial tactical dilemma in negotiations is who should go first? Is it better for the law firm to open with a particular position, or to ask the client to indicate the fee that they would be willing to pay? Most general negotiating text books recommend that it is best to persuade the other side to name the price first. This would enable the lawyer to gauge the ballpark that they are dealing with. Many experts on negotiation will suggest that even direct questions such as 'What would you charge for this matter?' should be deflected with the alternative question of 'How much are you willing to pay?'

Perhaps the more interesting topic for debate, is the question of when to start discussing the proposed fee. Baker asserts that "the sooner a firm quotes a price, the lower it will be". It is critical that the lawyer does not start discussing a price until the client is convinced of their value proposition. Baker suggests that if the client objects to the fee that has been quoted, "they may be doubting the value, not the price". Lawyers should postpone discussing any prices until they have obtained a full picture of the client's needs and the scope of work. They should then describe how the law firm will meet the client's needs and the benefits of working with the firm (remembering that it is preferable to elucidate the position through astute use of questions, rather than treating the client to a lengthy monologue on the virtues of the firm). If pressed by a client to name a figure at an early stage in negotiations, the lawyer can usually explain that they need to ask further exploratory questions first.

In the current economic climate, with so much emphasis on cost cutting, it is reasonable for lawyers to feel that they need to pare their prices to the bone in order to win business. However, experts in negotiating agree that it is much better to open with the highest price that the lawyer thinks could reasonably be achieved than to start at the lowest price that the lawyer is willing to accept. There is no chance of a lawyer securing a high price if he or she does not ask for it at the outset. However, any price quoted must be justifiable, in terms of the value to be provided to the client, or the lawyer will lose credibility. Indeed, reducing the price significantly without changing the service on offer will also have a negative impact, as is born-out by the comments of the legal procurement manager interviewed for Case study 3. This does not mean that the lawyer cannot offer a lower price to the client in a second round of negotiations, but the reduced price should be in exchange for a reduced or altered service, not because the law firm is simply accepting a reduced margin.

There are exceptions to the rule that law firms should aim high with their opening bid. Some clients run formal auction processes, either by choice or because they are bound by public procurement rules. If the client has stated that price is to be the prime consideration in such tender processes, then the firm has no choice but to bid low if it chooses to participate. Even in these circumstances, the firm will be able to ask questions in advance of submitting the bid. These questions can be used to establish the meaning of value for that client. Depending on the terms of the tender documents, the law firm may be able to emphasise value as a whole, rather than price in isolation. Alternatively, the law firm can focus on offering the core services required by the client, trim non-core areas or re-engineer delivery methods to make its services more economic.

Concessions and trades

It is normal to have to make some concessions during a negotiation but they do not have to be large. Even a small concession can make the client feel that it has achieved something. It is very common for parties to 'split the difference' but this may turn out to be a very bad deal and the implications should be worked through before it is agreed. When making a concession, a lawyer should always try to obtain something in return. For example, 'If we agree to a blended rate of £250 per hour, can you guarantee that you will instruct us on at least one new software licence agreement per month?' The firm may improve its overall position through such trading. An advantageous deal might be for the firm to offer to conduct all of the client's product liability work for a year for a flat fee, payable monthly. The firm will gain a guaranteed, regular income stream. This will improve its revenue, profit and cash flow positions at a stroke. It is therefore perfectly acceptable for the firm to charge a lower fee in exchange for these benefits than if it were to charge in arrears for time on the clock for conducting an equivalent amount of work.

Knowing that the client will be looking for the law firm to make some concessions in a negotiation, a lawyer can compile in advance a list of trades or fairly painless concessions which could be offered. Appendix 3 contains a checklist of easy trades that the lawyer can use for advance planning purposes. Any potential concessions should be held in reserve until they are needed. Paul Steele and Tom Beasor have written in their *Business Negotiation* workbook that "concessions are only valued if they are won".[8] They also advise that concessions offered by a client should never be rejected, even if they are not what the lawyer was looking for. Rejecting a concession causes offence. They counsel negotiators to "thank and bank" and then continue to ask for further concessions.

Concessions need not be made solely on price. Other variables which the law firm may find easier to move on, such as payment schedules and matter timetables or offering value-added services, may help the client to feel that they have obtained a good deal. As always, lawyers are recommended to ask their clients what they are most concerned about. It might be meeting a deadline or just knowing that a problem will be taken care of. The lawyer can then structure a trade accordingly.

Knowing when to walk away

As outlined in Chapter 8, it is imperative to prepare before entering a negotiation. The preparation will include identifying a preferred outcome and several alternative options which will also be acceptable to the firm. 'Success' must be defined in advance so that the lawyer has something to aim for. It is equally important to have established a walk-away point prior to entering the negotiation. It is all too easy to get carried away in the heat of the negotiation and to make concessions that render the job unprofitable if a back-stop position has not been established in advance of entering the negotiation. Determining the walk-away point involves more than a simple calculation of profit margins. Fisher and Ury coined the phrase "best alternative to a negotiated solution" or "BATNA". They urge negotiators to work out in advance of any negotiation what they will do if they cannot reach a negotiated settlement. For example, if the law firm does not win a place on the panel of a particular lending institution, then it would be able to continue to act on an *ad hoc* basis for corporate borrowers. Every cloud has a silver lining, as the saying goes. The better the BATNA, the more powerful the lawyer will feel in a negotiation. The lawyer might even choose to disclose the BATNA, as it may make the client realise the strength of the law firm's position.

Conversely, if the BATNA is very weak, then it may be worth the law firm's while to drop its prices below its ideal rate. Having a BATNA enables the lawyer to decide whether it is better to do a deal on the client's terms or to walk away. Fisher and Ury maintain that if you do not know your BATNA you are "negotiating with your eyes closed". The walk-away point – which will vary over time and may be different for each client and matter – is reached when the BATNA is more attractive than any negotiated settlement.

Closure

In order to know when to close a deal, a lawyer needs to know how to recognise success. This should be easy if the lawyer has prepared for the negotiation. When this stage is reached, the lawyer will need confirmation that the firm has been engaged and the terms agreed. Lawyers must of course be mindful of any professional obligations to provide their clients with details of the engagement terms, but they should also avoid high pressure sales tactics. These are notoriously unpopular with buyers of legal services. Clients often need time for reflection away from the negotiation meeting before making their minds up. If a final agreement has not been reached by the end of a negotiation session, the lawyer and client should at least agree next steps for moving the relationship or discussion forward and documenting it.

Tricks

Tricks to embrace

Silence

This is a powerful tool. Most people can't bear the tension and rush to fill a silence with a concession.

Time-out

If the lawyer is losing control of the discussion or a stalemate has been reached then a time-out can help. The break can be used to consult with colleagues, to marshal thoughts and to change the atmosphere. Alternatively, particularly thorny issues can be parked, while other more tractable topics are dealt with.

Tricks to use with caution

Threats

Issuing an ultimatum such as 'take it or leave it' or a threat such as 'that's a deal breaker' can be very effective when trying to bring a negotiation to a close, but it can also backfire, particularly if used too early or too often. If the client threatens to walk out, the lawyer should not capitulate. Instead, the lawyer should encourage the client to re-engage, perhaps after a time-out. The lawyer must resist rising to any bait and maintain a warm and friendly tone – for example, suggesting that the client might not want to walk out so close to the deal being finalised.

Tricks to avoid and watch out for

Good cop/bad cop

Perhaps the oldest trick in the book and therefore one that has to be mentioned is good cop/bad cop, where the good cop makes offers and the bad cop makes threats. This has become rather hackneyed and most people will see through it. Some skill and practice is also required to keep up the performance, so it is probably best avoided.

Nibbling

Nibbling is described by Nic Peeling as the tactic of demanding additional concessions after the deal was supposedly done. It doesn't reflect well on the nibbler.

Deferring to authority

Claiming lack of authority or blaming a third party, such as the managing partner, for an inability to reach agreement during a negotiation is poor form and will antagonise the client. If a lawyer's authority is genuinely limited then this should be made clear at the outset. This could result in the client refusing to negotiate until the person with authority is brought to the table. Likewise, if the client says that the chief executive or finance director will never approve such a fee, the lawyer can ask for the chief executive to be brought into the conversation directly. This will probably prompt the client, who will not want to drag the chief executive into such a discussion, to look for more creative solutions.

Bluffing

This is another word for lying. Some negotiators maintain that negotiation is a game and therefore lying is acceptable. It certainly isn't for lawyers. Not all clients will share these scruples.

Displays of temper

It is very important not to show strong emotion during a negotiation. Emotional outbursts look unprofessional and can cloud judgement.

Not playing

Some apparent negotiations are not really negotiations at all. If the client offers to pay a particular price and no more then it is not a negotiation. The lawyer can try to ask questions in order to enable the client to move onto a more productive discussion, but it may be a take it or leave it moment. Sometimes leaving it is the right thing to do. The lawyer will know which is the right decision if they have prepared well –

if they know their target fee and several alternatives, have established a BATNA, and determined their walk-away point.

If a counterparty displays bad behaviour, the lawyer should acknowledge it explicitly and then move-on, perhaps after a time-out to clear the air.

References

1. *Minding the Store*, Stanley Marcus, University of North Texas Press, Texas 1997
2. All references in this chapter to Ronald Baker are to *Implementing Value Pricing: A Radical Business Model for Professional Firms*, Ronald Baker, John Wiley & Sons, Inc., New Jersey, 2011
3. *Managing the Professional Service Firm*, David Maister, Simon & Schuster UK Ltd, 1993
4. *Just Ask The Right Questions To Get What You Want*, Ian Cooper, Pearson Education Ltd, Essex, 2007
5. *Brilliant Negotiations*, Nic Peeling, Pearson Education Ltd, Essex, 2nd Edition, 2011.
6. All references to Fisher and Ury in this chapter are to *Getting to Yes: Negotiating Agreement Without Giving In*, Roger Fisher and William Ury, Random Century Ltd, 2nd edition, London, 1991
7. eBusiness Master, *Body Language Basics – How to Quickly Recognise and Interpret the Signs and Signals*
8. All references in this chapter to Steele and Beasor are to *Business Negotiation, A Practical Workbook*, Paul Steele and Tom Beasor, Gower Publishing Limited, Hampshire 1999

Chapter 11: Developing a strategy for better budgeting and negotiating

"Knowing what to do is usually easy: doing it is hard." David Maister

THIS REPORT has so far examined why lawyers need to be able to create matter budgets and acquire and apply negotiating skills. It has then provided practical explanations and demonstrations of how to create and live within budgets, and negotiate effectively. The knowledge imparted can be applied by individual lawyers immediately but for firms which have relied upon after-the-event billing for as long as anyone can remember, significant changes to working practices may be required. For firm leaders, practice group and departmental heads, recognising that certain behaviours are desirable is only the starting point. Some firms have developed budgeting tools and made these available to fee earners but found that they are rarely used. Others have sent their fee earners on training courses in negotiating skills. These are admirable and necessary steps but they are not sufficient to ensure that fee earners will adopt the desired behaviours. As David Maister, one of the leading authorities on managing professional services firms, said in his book *Strategy and the Fat Smoker*,[1] "knowing what to do is usually easy: doing it is hard".

The final two chapters of this report are therefore written for those who are charged with changing the ways that their firms or departments operate in order for best-practice behaviour in budgeting and negotiating to become the norm. These individuals are referred to here as change leaders.

Before embarking on any kind of transformation programme, change leaders need first to analyse their firm's current position. Having understood where their firm is starting from they can develop realistic goals and a strategy for achieving them. The strategy must then be communicated throughout the firm and the lawyers within the organisation will need to be helped to change their ingrained habits and practices. Change leaders will encounter obstacles and frustrations along the way and must be able to maintain forward momentum over sustained periods. The end goal is that the great majority of the firm's lawyers are designing accurate matter budgets, working within these, and agreeing profitable fees with their clients – as a matter of habit. The remainder of this report tackles each stage of the transformation process.

Taking stock

Before endeavouring to make any changes within a firm, the change leader must understand the state that it is currently in. This includes the pervasive office culture and the behaviour currently exhibited by people within the firm.

Office culture

All offices have a culture. This has been very succinctly defined by two prominent academics from the University of Michigan, Kim Cameron and Robert Quinn,[2] as "how things are around here". Cameron and Quinn assert that the dominant culture of an organisation will tend to fall into one of the following four categories:

- Clan culture (like a family);
- Adhocracy (entrepreneurial);
- Hierarchy (policy and procedure driven); and
- Market (competitive).

Change leaders will need to assess the prevailing culture in their firm to determine which aspects of the culture may be inhibiting the adoption of better budgeting and negotiating behaviour. Each firm should be looked at on a case by case basis. If they are following Cameron and Quinn's framework, most law firms would recognise themselves as market cultures. These are tough and demanding environments; productivity is prized and there is a competitive atmosphere.

By contrast, many of the behaviours necessary to foster excellence in budgeting and negotiating are exhibited by organisations with a clan culture. Here team work is valued, commitment to the long term is a virtue, success is measured in terms of customer and employee satisfaction, and the firm's leaders act as mentors. A firm which is intent on offering AFAs to clients will find that old tendencies for individuals to compete for maximum hours billed or for ownership of a client are no longer desirable. Instead, sharing knowledge and delegating will help the firm to complete matters within the budgets that have been set.

It is rare for change leaders to be able to effect permanent behavioural change without commensurate adjustments in values and goals (in other words, culture change). Therefore, they may try to engender those elements of a clan culture which are likely to support the strategic objective of better budgeting and negotiating behaviour. However, when striving for culture change is it important not to 'throw the baby out with the bath water'. Market culture is not all bad, just as clan culture is not all good. Thus, a valid goal might be to empower employees, but this should not be at the expense of creating an overly permissive environment. Encouraging team playing within a firm should not crush the competitive spirit which drives the desire to perform better than other firms.

Behaviour

Again, before trying to instil individual behavioural change, it is necessary to be realistic about current behaviour. What this means in the context of achieving better budgeting and negotiating is set out below.

Better budgeting

If the goal is to ensure that fee earners create accurate matter budgets before commencing work on matters, then the change leader must first examine how matters are currently started. This will involve a review of:

- How instructions are received;
- The process and information required for opening new client and new matter files;
- How matter teams are assembled;
- The ways in which fee earners discuss fees with their clients and when these discussions take place;
- What resources and information are currently available to partners to enable them to forecast likely matter cost;
- To what extent partners make use of the available information and resources;
- Accuracy of the forecasts provided to clients;

- Where scope creep occurs and how fee earners handle it;
- The extent to which fee earners write-off time; and
- The length of time it takes to get paid after an invoice has been issued (counting the debtor days).

Better negotiating

If a change leader is intent on developing fee earners' negotiating skills so that the majority of matters achieve a desired minimum profit margin, this will involve a review of:

- The circumstances in which fee earners find themselves negotiating fees – for example, agreeing a fixed fee at the outset, a pre-agreed discount on all hourly rates for all matters conducted for particular clients, or discounting final bills;
- The most common negotiation forums – for example, face-to-face meetings, phone calls or email exchanges, and whether these involve multiple parties or bilateral discussions;
- The arguments put forward by clients in requesting discounts or chipping away at fees;
- The reasons that discounts are given;
- The size of discounts given;
- The actual impact of discounts on profit margin;
- The extent to which this is understood by fee earners during negotiations; and
- The ways in which fee earners prepare for negotiations, including whether they understand the cost to the firm of conducting the matter, the value to the client of the service being offered, and whether they establish several acceptable alternative positions and know their walk-away points before negotiations take place.

Having developed a clear vision of 'now', change leaders can move onto developing strategy for the future.

Developing and communicating vision and strategy

Vision

John Kotter, emeritus professor of leadership at Harvard Business School, says that leading change requires both a vision and a strategy.[3] The vision is the "picture of the future" whereas the strategy is the "logic for how the vision can be achieved". Kotter sets out the criteria for an effective vision as follows. The vision must be:

- Imaginable;
- Desirable;
- Feasible;
- Focused;
- Flexible; and
- Communicable.

In short, the vision will need to appeal to all stakeholders, which in the case of a law firm will mean partners, employees and clients. It should make the firm attractive to potential recruits and prospective clients and help to differentiate it from its competitors. The vision will need to take heed of the organisational culture (as described above), economic forces (such as the impact of the recession on clients) and other trends (such as commoditization of certain legal services.) A vision should be motivational and not too directional, allowing personnel some freedom of action in implementing the vision. Early and genuine involvement of staff at all levels in developing both the vision and the strategy, will pay dividends in terms of securing buy-in for the changes.

Developing a vision is likely to take time. One person, most probably the managing partner or a department head (depending on whether the vision is firm wide or focused on one practice group) will need to take the helm. However, vision needs what John Kotter refers to as a "guiding coalition" to steer it. The end result will be much richer, more realistic and more likely to be implemented as a result of having a knowledgeable and powerful group assisting the changer leader with its development. The change leader is bound to encounter opposition as vested interests are threatened. So, they will need to maintain focus and be undeterred by obstacles, whilst simultaneously taking account of stakeholder points of view.

Strategy

To generate a strategy from a vision, the change leader and guiding coalition need to perform a gap analysis – comparing where they want the firm to be, with where it is now. Then they must determine which behaviours, processes and systems underlie the firm's current culture and performance, and which alternative behaviours will stimulate the achievement of the vision for the firm's future.

Cameron and Quinn write that a "strategic action agenda" will set out the behaviours which the vision requires the firm to:

- Do more of;
- Start doing;
- Stop; or
- Continue as before.

The strategy will need to demonstrate the benefits that will accrue through change as contrasted with the disadvantages of maintaining the *status quo*. The proposed changes must be justified. When provided with reasons for change (or, better still, when involved early in brain-storming sessions from which the reasons for change emerge) members and employees of the firm will feel that they have been brought into the strategy-making process. This should make them less resistant to change. The strategy will need to focus on the processes needed both to effect the change and to adhere to the desired new best practices.

Communication

Having developed a vision and strategy, this must be communicated throughout the firm. As Jo Owen[4] says, "effective leadership communication is not about clearly stating what you think. Good communication requires thinking your way into the head of the other person". The change leader must consider the content, style and channels of communication.

Content

Owen draws inspiration from those renowned orators, the ancient Greeks, in listing the three constituents of communication as *logos, ethos* and *pathos*. In essence, communications must contain a logic (*logos*) which explains to people why they should pay attention to what is being said or written. Communications must contain a characteristic spirit which renders them believable (*ethos*) so the speaker or writer needs to find a way to achieve a bond with the audience. Finally, the communication must lead to an emotional connection with the recipient (*pathos*). This can be achieved through anecdotes which illustrate the points being made and bring them to life.

Style

The style of communication must be calculated to engage and inspire the audience. Owen again refers to "energy, enthusiasm and excitement... expertise and enjoyment". The change leader's thorough understanding of (and belief in) the project and determination to see it through must be evident.

Channels
Every communication channel available within the firm must be exploited in the communication effort. It is insufficient to explain change in a newsletter, which may not be read or believed. Briefing meetings, workshops, training sessions, intranets and chat forums must all be brought into play. Firms may consider taking 360-degree feedback and even changing physical symbols, such as the way that the work environment is laid out, corporate logos and mission statements.

Finally, it is absolutely essential that the change leader and senior partners within the organisation live the vision and, through their actions, leave no one in any doubt that they believe in the messages that they are disseminating across the firm.

References

1. All references in this chapter to David Maister are to *Strategy and the Fat Smoker*, David Maister, The Spangle Press, Boston, 2008
2. All references in this chapter to Cameron and Quinn are to *Diagnosing and Changing Organizational Culture: Based on the Competing Values Framework*, Kim Cameron and Robert Quinn, 3rd edition, Jossey-Bass, San Francisco, 2011
3. All references in this chapter to John Kotter are to *Leading Change*, John Kotter, Harvard Business School Publishing Corporation, Boston, 2008
4. All references in this chapter to Jo Owen are to *How to Lead*, 2nd edition, Jo Owen, Pearson Education Limited, Harlow, 2009

Chapter 12: Implementing change and embedding best practice

"What gets measured gets done." Traditional

HAVING ANALYSED office culture and behaviour, and then developed and communicated a vision and strategy for the firm or department, the change leader needs to tackle implementation. McKinsey identified "four conditions for changing individual mind-sets",[1] which in a law firm context mean that:

- Individuals must understand the reason for the change and agree with it;
- The firm's structures and systems must reinforce the sought after behaviours;
- Partners and employees must possess the skills needed to perform as expected; and
- Fee earners must have respected role models in the organisation on whom they can model their behaviour.

Leadership consultancy The Cognitas Group has combined these precepts with Ken Wilber's four quadrants[2] to define a set of change mechanisms, which change leaders can employ to bring about behavioural change. These are detailed in Figure 1. This chapter explains how the change mechanisms can be used to implement a strategy for budgeting and negotiating fees effectively with clients.

Developing personal insight

Each individual within the firm will need to understand the reasoning behind the new strategy and agree with it. This will be no mean feat to achieve. The change leader will need to be a powerful influencer, persuading the majority of partners and employees to change their minds about the way in which they conduct and price matters, and how they communicate with clients.

Jo Owen describes leadership as a team sport and says that the change leader must act as a sales person, which underlines the importance of creating a 'guiding coalition' to aid the sales effort as described in Chapter 11. For the change leader's message to be influential it will need to address:

- What the new practices should look like; and
- How adopting such practices will benefit the firm and each individual.

Messages will need to be tailored for the audience. The various constituents within the firm, such as trainees, partners and professional support lawyers, will have different anxieties and aspirations and will respond better to a vision and strategy which is crafted with their interests in mind. The interest groups themselves will not be homogeneous and the change leader will need to look out for individuals who are dragging their heels and seek ways to persuade them, to secure the success of the change project as a whole.

In practical terms, this can be achieved through a variety of means. Workshops, where small groups are guided through

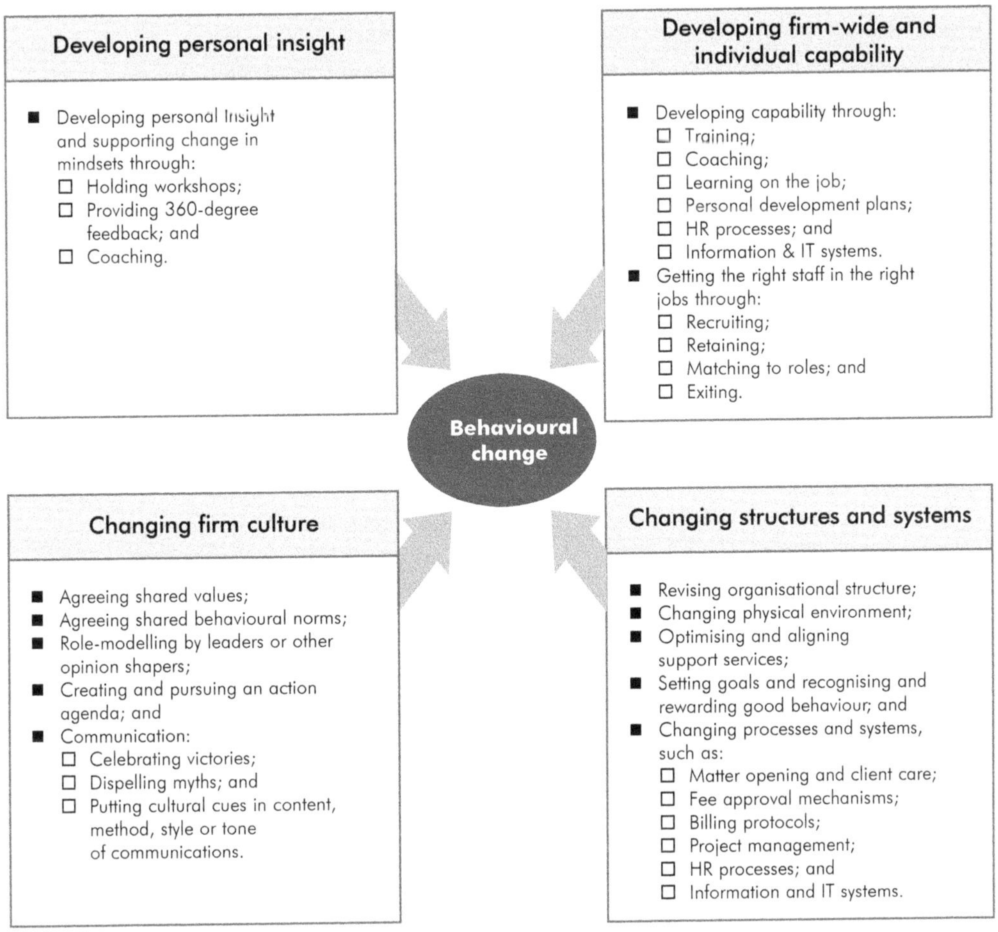

Figure 1: Change mechanisms
Adapted from materials provided by The Cognitas Group, with thanks

discussion and resolution of their concerns, and role-play scenarios can be helpful, as can coaching and mentoring. Individuals who are lacking in self-knowledge and do not perceive themselves as others do, can gain insights through 360-degree feedback from colleagues, as well as clients.

In seeking to influence firm members and employees, it is helpful for the change leader to be aware of the factors which are most likely to motivate and de-motivate people. A carrot and stick approach will probably be needed but attempts to influence by diktat alone will not win over hearts and minds. Being able to show tangible advantages for the individual in adhering to the plan will produce the greatest returns. These will flow through all the more readily if the change leader can make change easy to adopt. For example, if lawyers feel that they do not have the time or the skills to research and analyse historic matter billing data, then assigning this task to the KM team will overcome that obstacle.

Changing structures and systems

Changing structures can involve reorganising practice groups and reporting lines. Structures can also refer to the physical environment. Moving from single occupancy offices to an open-plan layout is an example of a structural change (the merits of which are the subject of strong debate) which can certainly have a dramatic influence on office atmosphere and team playing. Even changing branding can have a refreshing effect. However, when it comes to implementing best-practice budgeting and negotiating, the spotlight will most likely fall on firm systems. In particular, aligning support services functions and reward and recognition systems with the firm's strategy will be essential, if a firm is to deliver its vision of better budgeting and negotiating.

Optimising and aligning support services

Fee earners are the public face of law firms but below the radar, particularly in larger firms, an army of often unsung heroes in the support services labours to facilitate the smooth running of the firm. The support functions will typically include finance, HR, IT, KM and business development (BD). In large firms, the number of support personnel may equal the number of fee earners. Each of these functions has a role in cultivating best-practice budgeting and negotiating within law firms.

Finance

The finance team is likely to be the repository of historic financial data which can be used in budget planning. It prepares the management accounts, which will be used by the firm, departments and individuals to assess the profitability of their work. The team may help fee earners to assess the potential profitability of their proposed budgets, or it may take responsibility for overseeing the creation of budgeting tools for use by fee earners. A word of caution here: any tools designed for use by fee earners must be developed in consultation with fee earners and must be thoroughly road-tested by those destined to use them, or they will simply not be used. The firm's existing financial reporting tools can also be adapted to enable fee earners and firm leaders to monitor how well they are adhering to matter budgets. The most popular financial reporting tools used by law firms, such as Elite and Crystal Reports, can provide a degree of budget-to-performance monitoring.

IT

The IT department is likely to work alongside the finance team in creating or procuring any budgeting tools – whether these are designed specifically for the law firm or are purchased off the shelf from third-party suppliers, such as LexisNexis, Aderant or Thomson Reuters.

KM

Matter templates will most probably be developed by the KM team, which may also take the lead in analysing both historic matter fee information and new intelligence that is produced as a by-product of ongoing matters. In many firms, the time-recording systems were designed to generate invoices rather than to enable easy matter cost comparisons to be made. As a result, the process of deriving meaningful data from historic time entries can be a painstaking task, for which fee earners do not have time. Some tools being brought to market for this purpose, such as the Matter Experience Module from LexisNexis, may simplify this task. Most obviously, the KM team will have a vital role to play in providing training for fee earners at all levels within the firm. This will include a range of topics to complement the firm's budgeting and negotiating strategy, such as understanding law firm finance, negotiating skills, and how to use the various budgeting tools that are available.

BD

Pricing a matter is not solely about plugging numbers into a financial model. The price that a firm is prepared to offer a client may depend on other strategic considerations, such as the growth potential of that client. The price that will actually be achieved will also be reliant on the success of the negotiation. Chapter 7 was devoted to how to manage the negotiation process. It emphasised the importance of preparation before entering a negotiation. Preparation in this context includes understanding value from the client's perspective as well as performing an analysis of the client. This should establish the client's strategic importance to the firm, what they are like to work with, how they fit with the firm's strategic goals (for example, to break into a new geography or practice area) and the likely pipeline of work coming from them. While the client relationship partner may know this information better than anyone, the BD team can provide useful summaries and analysis. It should also be recognised that creating matter budgets is not every fee earner's strong point. The ambition, over time, should be to create more capable fee earners. In the short term, BD professionals may be brought in to help fee earners to create matter budgets. This has happened at Crowell & Moring (see Case study 2).

HR

The HR team's remit involves recruitment, reward, retention and removal of fee earners. When looking for new recruits, one of the criteria upon which they should be judged is their commercial astuteness and willingness to adopt the practices which the firm is seeking to nurture. Fee earners need to be motivated to adopt best practices. Motivation comes from many sources, some intrinsic and some extrinsic, but reward and remuneration are obvious factors and are described in more detail below. Appraisal processes and criteria upon which fee earners are judged need to reflect the store set by the firm on good budgeting and negotiating behaviour. Finally, despite the firm's best efforts to develop individuals through training and personal development plans, it is inevitable that some fee earners will be unable or unwilling to adapt to the new paradigm. The HR team will need to have robust policies and procedures for managing out such individuals.

Each function needs to play its part in cultivating best-practice budgeting and negotiating among the fee earners, but there is also crossover between the departments, where lines are blurred and teams need to co-operate. For example, the finance function may record the profitability of historic matters, the IT department may build the database on which such information is stored and the KM team may roll out training on understanding the numbers and using the database.

Recognising and rewarding good behaviour

In the natural order of things, good behaviour should be rewarded. As Phil Gott[3] says, "what gets rewarded gets repeated". Rewards are designed to:

- Attract and retain top quality personnel;
- Encourage behaviour which will improve the firm's financial performance; and
- Promote other key objectives destined to enhance the long-term fortune of the firm.

In the law firm context, this is often taken to mean financial reward in the form of salary, bonus or profit share, but firms are divided on the wisdom of providing financial reward for individual performance. Some consider it divisive because it can lead to an erosion of team work and a short-term outlook. Not all firms operate bonus mechanisms and in many firms (particularly in the UK) salary and profit shares are based on a lock-step system (compensation based on firm performance and seniority rather than personal merit). In firms where individual performance is not rewarded in monetary terms, good behaviour can still be rewarded by other means. This might be in the form of more intellectually stimulating work, a more high-profile client or, of course, promotion. Even where a formal promotion is unavailable, many studies have shown that professionals thrive when they are trusted with increasingly interesting and challenging work. They also appreciate learning and development and other opportunities for personal growth.

In order to distribute rewards, firms need some kind of mechanism for recognising good performance. Some of this will be informal. Particularly at partner level, some firms still operate very opaque criteria for reward, which remains at the discretion of the managing partner or an elite cabal of partners. However, most firms have instituted a system of formalised appraisals to take place at least once per year, particularly for junior staff. There will be firms where appraisals are permanently delayed in order to give priority to client work or where the appraisal is no more than a box-ticking exercise. This is a wasted opportunity. Used correctly, appraisals can play a very significant role in directing lawyers' performance. Training in the proper conduct of appraisals is vital if this tool is to be used as an effective lever of change.

Advantages of formal appraisal systems are that, in addition to being transparent and fair, they also force the firm to think carefully about what kind of behaviour is being rewarded. The old saying, 'what gets measured gets done' is very apposite. Firms should think very carefully about the basis upon which decisions to grant reward are made. As the Russian scientist Pavlov famously observed, expectations and behaviour are conditioned by past experience. Pavlov was able to induce salivation in dogs by the mere ringing of a bell, as the sound of the bell had become the signal for food. If billing the greatest number of hours has always led to the largest bonus or the fastest track to promotion then lawyers will continue to view the pursuit of the largest number of billable hours as their primary goal.

The firm needs to consider what it is paying its lawyers to do and then clearly outline the targets which they must meet in order to secure reward. In most firms, this still takes the form of a billable hours target, but if a firm is seeking to introduce better budgeting and negotiating behaviour then such targets are likely to conflict with the firm's strategic goals. Billable hours targets are beautifully simple and this, combined with a historic overemphasis on top-line revenue rather than bottom-line profits has led to the pre-eminence of billable hours targets for lawyers. However, they are certainly not the only valid measures of lawyer performance – nor, indeed, are they the correct measures for those adopting AFAs. Some firms are now taking steps to set alternative targets. *The Lawyer* recently reported that Nabarro (a UK commercial law firm) has "increased its emphasis on soft factors such as keeping clients happy and sourcing new work when slicing up equity to partners".[4] The fact that this was worthy of reporting shows that this is still a relatively uncommon practice but it can (and should) be done.

Developing firm wide and individual capability

Learning

As discussed above, members and employees of the firm will need to be trained in law firm finance, matter profitability, budget creation, project management and negotiating skills if the firm's vision is to become reality. Controversially, David Maister[5] has declared that most "training is useless" despite earning his shilling (or rather, dollar) for many years by training lawyers and other professionals. In *Strategy and the Fat Smoker*, Maister goes on to explain that it is not the principle of training which is at fault, but the way in which it is carried out or the timing of it. On the latter point, in Maister's view, "training is a wonderful *last* step in bringing about changed organisational and personal behaviour, but a pathetically useless *first* step". It is no use training people if the systems and structures have not first been changed in order to make it easy for everyone to put that training into practice.

The next few paragraphs deal with how training can be conducted to achieve optimal results. The word training is in fact a somewhat narrow term and is often replaced with the broader definition of learning and development. This shifts the focus from the traditional view of training as something which is classroom based (the download of information from a lecturer to a passive audience) to something which suggests much more active involvement and commitment from the person who is learning. Just as everyone in the firm needs to buy into its vision, and the change leaders need to use their influencing skills to make this happen, so training based on telling people what to do is less effective than methods which help influence a change in beliefs.

Types of learning

Learning is about acquiring knowledge but it may also be about building skills or altering attitudes. Lawyers can acquire knowledge by being provided with facts and through repetition. They can build skills and change their attitudes by being given the opportunity to practice and experiment in a safe learning environment. Where attitudes are concerned, old beliefs need to be whittled away before new ideas can be implanted and then reinforced with examples and anecdotes.

Learning styles

Much has been written about learning styles perhaps most influentially by David Kolb, whose writing was developed into practical tools by Peter Honey and Alan Mumford.[6] This has been usefully summarised by Phil Gott in the Ark report, *Learning and Development in Law Firms*. To name just two possibilities, some people learn better by watching, others by doing. Just as change leaders will need to tailor the communication of their vision to suit their audience, so too a menu of different training methods can be made available to cater for individual learning styles.

Learning methods

Classroom learning certainly has a role to play but other methods include:

- Web – online training modules can be downloaded by individuals at a time and location that suits them. They may have interactive elements such as quizzes to check that learning goals have been achieved and the person in charge of the training can monitor usage and provide feedback to management when the learning module has been completed. The options opened up by the web are continually increasing. Reading, writing and participating in blogs, podcasts, wikis and social networks can all be utilised. Virtual worlds, such as Second Life, can be used for extended and repeated situation simulations, such as fee negotiation scenarios.

- Mentoring – mentors can supplement formal training. They tend to be experienced and skilled individuals drawn from within the firm, who can share their experience and guide lawyers who are developing their budgeting and negotiating skills.
- Coaching – this is most often conducted by an external professional. A coach is trained to help individual lawyers to fulfil their potential. By asking questions, the coach helps the lawyers to become more self-aware and to work out their own solutions and tactics.
- Work experience – some of the most powerful learning is done 'on the job'. The lessons learned in this way are sometimes painful but they tend never to be forgotten. Once a lawyer has received formal training in skills and tools, and has observed and worked alongside a more experienced colleague, the firm needs to give that lawyer some scope to put theory into practice. Budgets won't always be right and negotiations won't always go entirely to plan. But if firms want to build capability in all their lawyers (rather than reserving budgeting and negotiating for a specialist individual or team) then they must trust their lawyers and give them a degree of autonomy. Where early attempts do not go to plan, the consequence should be further learning rather than criticism.

Appraisals

Phil Gott reports that "up to 80 per cent of under-performance in the workplace arises from lack of effective feedback being provided". Therefore it is vital that law firms have in place appraisal systems which capture information about fee earners' performance in the areas which the firm is trying to develop – in this case, budgeting and negotiating skills. Many people are now familiar with 360-degree feedback, where a lawyer's more senior and junior colleagues and peers are asked to contribute their constructive criticism of the lawyer's performance for the purposes of an appraisal. More unusually, but particularly useful in the law firm context, clients may also be asked to submit their comments. Appraisals have two functions. One is to provide a basis for decisions on pay, bonuses and promotions. More is said about this aspect of appraisals in the section of this report on recognising and rewarding good behaviour. The other purpose of appraisals is to enable firms to identify areas of weakness and to create personal development plans for each lawyer so that each lawyer can be helped to achieve improved performance. This is discussed below.

Personal development plans

Where law firms have visions and strategies, individuals should have agreed personal development plans which provide the route map for progression to the next stage in their career, or to the achievement of other performance objectives. Information gleaned from appraisals together with lawyers' own ambitions can be turned into actionable recommendations. A personal development plan is likely to list specific steps to be taken and milestones to be achieved in the coming year, with some looser aspirations for achievements over perhaps the next three to five years.

At the next appraisal, the lawyer's success in following the personal development plan can be reviewed. The findings will impact both reward and the revised goals that are set for the following year. Throughout the year, lawyers can refer to their own development plans to remind themselves of how they should be behaving and to monitor their own progress.

Recruitment, retention and exiting

Developing capability is much easier if the talent pool has been rigorously selected with the desired attributes in mind. Interviews and assessments of potential new recruits should reveal candidates' attitudes to, and experience of, budgeting and negotiating with clients. Persistent non-conformers should be managed out of the firm in accordance with rigorous but fair and well-publicised processes.

Changing firm culture

Chapter 11 dealt with how to evaluate a firm's existing culture, in order to be able to develop a realistically achievable vision for the future. Changing office culture will involve:

- Recognising and reaching agreement on the current office culture and what the future should look like;
- Agreeing shared values and expected behaviours;
- Leaders acting as role models;
- Training, coaching and mentoring;
- Creating and sticking to an action agenda;
- Achieving early quick wins and celebrating success;
- Maintaining accountability by developing metrics and milestones against which to measure achievement; and
- Communication at multiple levels.

Agreeing cultural goals, values and behaviours

Members of the firm and employees will be much more accepting of change if they feel involved in the decision making behind the strategy and the process of implementing it. As outlined above, when communicating the vision and strategy, it is necessary to start by outlining the problem that the firm is seeking to fix, such as:

- Too much time written off due to scope creep;
- Unacceptable delays in fees being paid, meaning that the firm has to incur expensive overdraft charges; or
- Being unable to operate fixed fees profitably.

The change leader should then appeal to partners and staff for help in bringing about the change and invite proposals as to how the leadership can help them to help the firm to realise the vision.

Role models

Junior personnel will tend to mimic the behaviour of their more senior colleagues. If senior partners within the firm ignore the change initiative because their ways of working have become too entrenched, then more junior staff cannot be expected to practice what is being preached but not observed. Firm leaders will need the courage to confront and manage partners exhibiting such detrimental behaviour.

Creating and sticking to an action agenda and establishing 'quick wins'

As with any other project, there needs to be a clearly worked out programme of actions to be taken in order to convert the ideals espoused in the vision to a practical reality. The agenda should contain specific, measurable and time-bound tasks. It is important for morale and maintaining momentum that some of these tasks should deliberately be designed as quick wins. Successes can then be celebrated and publicised throughout the firm. Success will breed further success (unless complacency sets in).

Communication

The strategy, shared values, expected behaviours and progress towards achieving the firm's goals can never be over-communicated. The style and tone of communications will be as important as the content in conveying the true attitudes and beliefs of the firm's senior managers.

Delivering success

Why change programmes often fail

Many readers will be daunted by the prospect of embarking on any kind of change programme, partly because they will have witnessed the failure of many worthy attempts at change in their firms and elsewhere. One frequent pitfall is for the change leader to announce the programme with an initial fanfare, only to fail to follow-up on its delivery. John Kotter[7] has analysed why so many transformation programmes fail. His findings can be summarised as:

- Change leaders are too complacent – Kotter says that "too much past success, a lack of visible crises, low performance standards, insufficient feedback from external constituencies" can all lead to complacency. When complacency sets in, the change programme drifts along and after a while is quietly ignored.
- The change leader has failed to assemble a guiding coalition – if influential partners do not support and actively participate in the change programme then the change leader will be undermined at every step of the process.
- There is an insufficiently compelling vision and it is under-communicated – the importance of creating a vision and then communicating it has been discussed above and in Chapter 11.
- The change programme has become mired in obstacles – there are always multiple hurdles to be vaulted during the change process. Some will be anticipated at the start of the programme and others will appear unexpectedly. Firm structure and reward systems, for example, must not be allowed to obstruct the change programme.
- A failure to create 'quick wins' – change programmes are often multi-year efforts. It is hard for all concerned to maintain their enthusiasm over such a long period. Individuals will need to see some payback for the effort that they are expending in pursuit of the vision. Quick wins help to maintain enthusiasm and belief but the change leader must create them rather than just hoping for them.
- Victory is declared too soon – rather like a builder who never quite completes the snagging list, it is tempting for the change leader to graduate from the change programme to new tasks when the end is in sight, only to find that the change programme falters and even goes backwards.
- Corporate culture remains unchanged – as discussed earlier in this chapter, change cannot be expected to take hold if the firm's culture militates against it.

Troubleshooting

The change leader is bound to encounter people and processes which are seemingly destined, by accident or design, to thwart change. There will be times when conflict seems inevitable. Just as some lawyers shy away from entering fee negotiations with clients, many firm leaders fear conflict, particularly where they are rarely in a position to dictate how their fellow partners should behave. Avoiding conflict will not solve anything. However, it should be handled carefully. Conflict does not have to be made personal. As when negotiating with clients, the key is to focus on issues and interests rather than emotions. The change leader needs to take a creative approach, forging options which will ameliorate the blocker's concerns. The change leader does not need to act in isolation. This is another example of where the guiding coalition can be instrumental in either providing suggestions to the change leader or influencing the blocker to mend their ways.

Maintaining momentum

In change management circles, there is a well-recognised concept called the change curve. A variant of this, developed by leadership consultants The Cognitas Group, working in conjunction with Jo Owen, is shown in Figure 2. It likens the change curve to a journey which commences at 'Lake placid'. The programme may stall at the outset due to complacency. This needs to be avoided by establishing and communicating the need for change and building enthusiasm for the change programme. Failure to do so is likely to lead to a slide into the 'Valley of death'. Here, all the changes which have been wrought have only made life at the firm (also known as profitability or client relationships) worse than it was before. Fatigue, frustration and despair set in. At this point, it is important to acknowledge the negative emotions that are being felt, to recognise the obstacles in the path and to reinvigorate the change plan. If this is done, the worst phase will be passed through and the firm will continue on the 'Trek to success'. There may be ups and downs and the going may be tough but, if the change leader steers a steady pace, keeping deviations in check, then gradually the firm will mount the 'Summit of satisfaction'. Here, they should take justifiable pride in their success but be wary not to slip back into complacency.

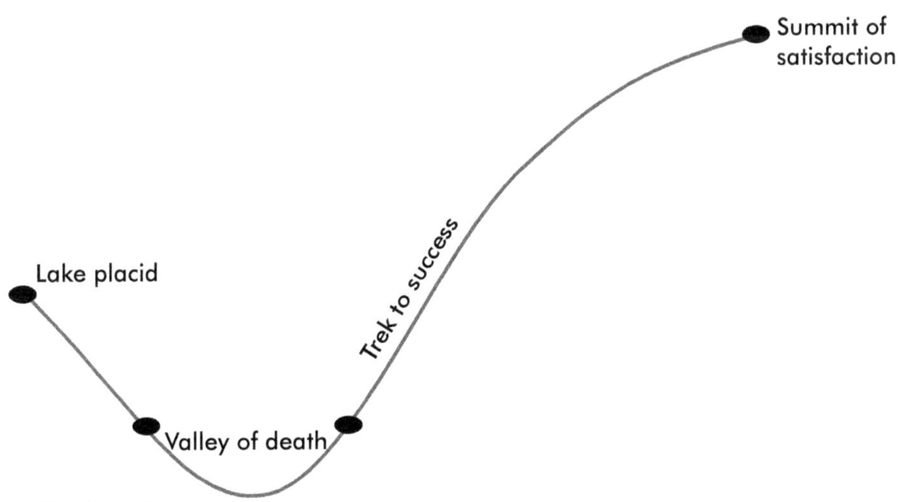

Figure 2: The change journey
Adapted from materials provided by The Cognitas Group/Jo Owen, with thanks

Embedding best-practice budgeting and negotiating will involve the firm undergoing a process of change at both the individual and the firm level. The change journey will include helping individual fee earners to understand why change is important; encouraging individual efforts through firm-wide systems and structures which support the desired behaviours; guiding fee earners' personal development through training, coaching and mentoring; and by bringing in and retaining personnel with the appropriate skills. Finally, by creating an optimal firm culture in which the desired behaviours can thrive.

Once structures have been aligned with the strategy, unhelpful senior members of the firm have been converted to the cause or eased-out, and fee earners' skills have been developed, the partners and employees of the firm should be singing from the same hymn sheet and take pride in delivering the shared vision.

References

1. 'The Psychology of Change Management', Emily Lawson and Colin Price, *The McKinsey Quarterly*, 2003 *Special Edition: The Value in Organization*
2. *The Integral Vision: A Very Short Introduction to the Revolutionary Integral Approach to Life, God, the Universe and Everything*, Ken Wilber, Shambhala, Boston and London, 2007
3. All references in this chapter to Phil Gott are to *Learning and Development in Law Firms*, Phil Gott, Ark Conferences Ltd, London 2010
4. 'Nabarro adds 'softer' element to partner pay', Joshua Freeman, *The Lawyer*, http://www.thelawyer.com, 28 July 2011
5. All references to David Maister in this chapter are to *Strategy and the Fat Smoker*, David Maister, The Spangle Press, Boston, 2008
6. http://www.peterhoney.com
7. All references in this chapter to John Kotter are to *Leading Change*, John Kotter, Harvard Business School Publishing Corporation, Boston, 2008

PART TWO

Case studies

Case study 1: DMH Stallard LLP – Business tools for budgeting, negotiating and client communication

Based on an interview with Tim Aspinall, managing partner

DMH STALLARD LLP is a top-100 UK law firm with offices in London and South East England. With over 50 partners, the firm provides a full range of legal services with particular strengths in corporate, commercial, banking, intellectual property, dispute resolution, property, planning, employment and private client. DMH Stallard acts for larger private companies, public companies, public sector organisations and private clients. The firm prides itself on its businesslike approach to project delivery and has implemented a range of business tools to enable the firm to be open and transparent when agreeing fees with clients. Using the same tools, DMH Stallard is able to keep clients informed of any delays, problems or important milestones. Its success in this field was publicly recognised in 2009, when the firm won the MPF European Practice Management Award for 'best use of technology'.

Tim Aspinall is managing partner at the firm and was appointed in 1997. Since that time, he has overseen growth in turnover from £6m per year to £25m.

The business tools

Project plans

DMH Stallard has developed project plans, which show the various tasks to be performed on any matter and the appropriate timetables for these tasks, in the form of a Gantt chart (a bar chart that illustrates a project schedule). The chart is accompanied by a narrative, which assigns responsibility for each task.

Budget templates

These are a form of financial model. The budget template identifies the tasks to be performed on any matter. These will replicate those shown on the project plans. Whereas the project plans focus on the timetable, the budget templates show the number of hours to be worked, by whom and their charge-out rates. Figures for expected matter cost to the firm, fee income and profitability are all included. The budget template is pre-populated with formulae so that a change in any of the parameters, such as the number of hours worked by a partner, will automatically flow through to the final profitability figure. The budget templates are similar to the matter budget template provided in Appendix 2.

Process maps

Process maps show workflows. They are mainly used for more repetitive types of work. They ensure that the matter teams work consistently and efficiently by following pre-set paths and actions. The process maps link to DMH Stallard's case management and document management systems.

DMH Direct

DMH Direct is a sophisticated extranet which is made available, often free of charge, to the firm's clients. It provides detailed management information to enable clients to track the progress of matters both in terms of milestones achieved and fees. DMH Direct has additional facilities, which enable clients to provide instructions to the firm or to access documents online.

How the tools were developed

When Aspinall began work as a lawyer he was surprised by how opaque fee discussions were. He felt lawyers were generally poor at pricing and, on becoming managing partner, was determined that DMH Stallard would take a more sophisticated approach. In particular, Aspinall was keen to be able to operate on the basis of fixed fees as much as possible. In order to do so, the firm had to be able to create reliable budgets.

Aspinall did not initially envisage launching a suite of tools. He began with process maps, then budget templates. He found that they were linked and the range of business tools grew to fit the need. The firm's lawyers built the business tools themselves with help from the IT support team. They did not use external consultants to any great degree. This may have prolonged the process, but meant that the tools were tailored to the requirements of the firm and its clients.

It took a lot of hard work to develop the business tools over a number of years. Aspinall's original intention was that lawyers should review their historic matters to establish the ideal resource and time requirements for each matter. In practice, in a buoyant market with work flooding in, the DMH Stallard lawyers were just too busy to go through this rather painstaking process. Nonetheless, they began to create budgets for matters. Inevitably there was a degree of trial and error. Once a matter completed, the lawyers found it relatively simple to look back at the budget and pinpoint the areas where there was a difference between the expected and actual time spent. They were then able to apply this intelligence to subsequent matters and improve the accuracy of their budgets.

Implementation

Implementation was another matter. Getting lawyers to use the new business tools was not easy and Aspinall estimates that it took around three years for the business tools to gain widespread acceptance. "Lawyers are very task driven," he says. "They didn't want the hassle. They just wanted to start the next job and complete it." Many lawyers also started out with the mindset that budget templates, process maps and project plans were for other people because each of their jobs was unique. "Lawyers often feel that it undermines their self-esteem to say that they are just part of a process," says Aspinall. "They have this idea that it is all a very intuitive and personal process rather than one that you could write down." Over time, Aspinall was able to demonstrate that even the largest corporate matters followed a basic process.

The solution was to find champions – people who were willing to use the new business tools and would then act as advocates for them within the firm. Aspinall's first champion was a litigator. Once the business tools were gaining traction in the litigation department, he moved on to the corporate department and created a champions team there. Now there are many partners within the firm leading by example, which means more junior staff automatically follow because best practice is embedded in the culture of the firm.

Finally, all lawyers are given plenty of training both in how to use the business tools and in the financial principles which underpin them. The firm publishes a great deal of financial information internally. Personal and team targets are set and publicised. Any lawyer can check their individual or team performance on the intranet, which is known as the 'BUS' (for its 'bloody useful statistics'). This helps partners and staff to understand the impact of their actions on the firm's financial performance.

Impact on the firm

Adoption of AFAs

Currently, approximately 50 per cent of the work undertaken by DMH Stallard is on the basis of fixed fees.

Businesslike approach

The main benefit to the firm has been that the introduction of the business tools has led to a wholesale culture shift. The firm now approaches new instructions in a businesslike manner. The mantra is 'on time, on budget, no surprises'. Aspinall is confident that the firm's lawyers now understand the firm's finances and can operate AFAs profitably.

Alignment of expectations

The existence of project plans and budget templates forces partners to set out how much time they believe should be spent on a matter. This information can be usefully communicated with both internal team members and clients. Where previously they worked in a vacuum and may have recorded hours that could never be recovered, junior lawyers are now guided as to the amount of time that they should reasonably devote to a task. Before a matter commences, the client can be consulted on the plan. At this stage, they can choose to re-focus the priorities or to take on more or less responsibility for certain tasks which may lead to an adjustment of price. The critical features are that the client is given choice and supports the decisions taken. DMH Stallard is able to discuss risks and needs openly with clients to come to an acceptable arrangement, which balances budget and time constraints against risk.

Increased business and enhanced client relationships

When tendering for new business, Aspinall finds that the business tools demonstrate to clients that the firm is efficient and innovative. He believes that the business tools have a positive but not decisive impact on hiring decisions, which are made on the basis of an evaluation of a complex mix of factors. Once appointed to a panel, the transparency, certainty and efficiency created by the business tools can all lead to the firm being instructed more often. Clients also have a greater appreciation of the work that the firm conducts on their behalf.

Successful negotiation of profitable business

The business tools really make themselves felt in the negotiating arena. Lawyers can use them to establish their negotiating positions and walk-away points. The business tools enable them to justify their prices to clients based on reasoned arguments. If an initial price is not right, by engaging with the client and using the business tools, the planned scope of work, delivery model or service standards can be easily adjusted to achieve a price point that is acceptable to both the firm and the client.

Although the business tools were designed for creating a realistic budget, Aspinall notes that certain types of work have a market price. The business tools enable DMH Stallard's lawyers to assess whether such matters can be conducted profitably. Where the firm has won work in these circumstances, the lawyers have been able to reverse-engineer the business tools and work back from the market price, to establish how to complete the matters within the fee constraints.

Continuous improvement and challenges for the future

Aspinall acknowledges the inherent tension between lawyers' fee-earning targets and the drive towards efficient working practices dictated by AFAs. DMH Stallard lessens this potential conflict by rewarding lawyers based on their fee earning rather than their hours recorded. The firm's lawyers understand that, "It's the amount of time that's converted to fees that counts," says Aspinall. And they are not incentivised to over record.

Even at DMH Stallard there isn't 100 per cent take up, but the business tools are very widely used. Aspinall has found that lawyers struggle most with the project plans, which they don't all take to intuitively. He is now looking to enhance the reward and incentive structure to reflect the value placed by the firm on efficient working and sticking to budgets.

Even with simple to use and effective business tools, it is not always possible to quote a fixed fee at the outset for an entire matter, but the firm can at least break the process down into phases and quote before the start of each one.

Inevitably, even when all the business tools are deployed, matters are sometimes subject to scope creep. This could be for a wide variety of reasons, such as an obstructive third party or a client changing priorities. Thanks to the budget templates, process maps and project plans, DMH Stallard lawyers have a fine appreciation of a matter's scope and know when it has been exceeded. A challenge still to be conquered is ensuring that lawyers raise the issue of scope creep with the client as soon as it arises rather than waiting for the more convenient or appropriate moment, which is unlikely to come.

Naturally, some lawyers are better at pricing and scoping work than others. Aspinall has recently introduced a policy whereby all new fixed price matters beyond a certain threshold have to be run past one of the firm's acknowledged experts in pricing and scoping. "Partners are happy to share knowledge if it increases performance," says Aspinall. Gradually, more DMH Stallard lawyers will develop the necessary pricing and scoping expertise and will be able to act independently.

Case study 2: Crowell & Moring LLP – Using AFAs and value-based billing

Based on an interview with Robert Lipstein, partner and leader of the firm's value-based billing initiatives

CROWELL & MORING LLP was founded in 1979, by a group of lawyers from a major law firm, who wanted to create a new firm which prioritised team working and innovation. The firm now has over 500 lawyers practising across the US and in London and Brussels. It is currently ranked 81st in the *American Lawyer's* AmLaw 100 list of the US' largest law firms (based on gross revenue). The firm is particularly well known for its litigation and arbitration, regulatory and transactional matters.

Robert Lipstein is a partner in Crowell & Moring's antitrust, international investment, trade and arbitration (ITA) and intellectual property groups. He is chair of the firm's finance and contingent fee review committees and leads the firm's value-based billing initiatives.

Alternative fees used by Crowell & Moring

Crowell & Moring began introducing AFAs more than a decade ago. The firm states that "we no longer consider these 'alternative' but as our primary fee arrangements". Its innovative approach was recognised in the *Financial Times*, when it won the *FT* Innovative Lawyers Award 2009 for its billing and fee arrangements. AFAs are tailored to suit clients' needs but may include any of the following:

- Blended rates – a single rate regardless of the status of the lawyer carrying out the work;
- Caps – fees will not exceed the amount of the cap;
- Collars – a fee is agreed but is surrounded by a collar, which allows variation within an agreed range according to time on the clock. Outside the collar, the client and the law firm share the savings or the overruns in agreed proportions;
- Credits towards new business – reduced fees on one matter in exchange for the client using the firm in a new area;
- Holdbacks – an agreed percentage of the bill is held back but in return the firm can earn a bonus worth a multiple of the holdback as a reward for excellence;
- Success fees – a performance bonus;
- Phase-based fees – the matter is broken down into phases and most commonly a fixed fee is charged for each one;
- Contingency fees – depending on local regulatory requirements. These might take the form of no-win no-fee litigation when acting for a plaintiff. But also, reverse contingency arrangements when acting for a defendant where, if the firm can resolve the matter for less than the exposure attributed to it by the client, then the firm will be paid an agreed percentage of the client's savings; and
- Value billing – where the firm is paid in accordance with the value ascribed to

the matter by the client as discussed in more detail below.

Genesis of AFAs at the firm

Crowell & Moring began by offering contingency fees on anti-trust recovery litigation. Lipstein describes these as "the ultimate in AFAs" as they are entirely dependent on success. Subsequently, around 2005, a client started to insist that all its external counsel introduce a system of holdbacks. Lipstein says that Crowell & Moring saw this as "a terrific opportunity to show the client that we were strategic and creative".

Following on from the success of this initiative, the firm decided to roll out the idea to a number of other existing clients with which it already had broad relationships. Lipstein says that the clients were intrigued to find "a law firm that was willing to put a portion of its compensation in the discretionary hands of the client". It was not long before Crowell & Moring determined to make AFAs part of its business model. AFAs are now offered to new clients as well as existing ones.

The introduction of AFAs was pioneered and driven at the highest management level within the firm and is strongly supported by its chairman, Kent Gardiner. The leadership's staunch belief in AFAs resonated with partners and fee earners who then took up the cause. The firm's first attempts at AFAs were hugely successful and this acted as a spur to the adoption of AFAs across the firm.

Spotlight on value billing

Defining value billing

Value billing implies that the firm's incentives are aligned with the client's. The focus is on outputs, or what has been achieved for the client, as opposed to inputs, which are the number of hours worked. The guiding ethos of value fees is that the firm's financial success should be determined more by clients' perceptions of the value created and less by the level of effort expended by the firm.

Determining the fee

The starting point for the creation of a value fee is always a discussion with the client. The firm needs to ask the client what constitutes a win in their eyes and what their goals are. These might be:

- Certainty of spend;
- Speed of resolution;
- A pre-determined spend to value ratio; or
- Obtaining the services of the most experienced lawyers for 'bet the company' work.

Crowell & Moring has built a module into its intake process so that as a new matter or new client file is opened, the economics of the proposed AFA can be modelled. The financial model will reflect who will carry out the work, how many hours work will be involved and will analyse the resultant profitability of the matter. This is similar to the processes described in Chapter 5 of this report, which are further illustrated by the financial modelling tools in Appendices 1 and 2.

At Crowell & Moring, the financial model will be sent to a member of the finance and contingent fee review committee for review. In addition to the pure financial analysis, they will consider the firm's strategic objectives in regard to the particular client or matter. Lipstein's team will take cognisance, for example, of whether the matter is to be performed for a new client or an existing client providing instructions in a new area of practice.

Once the pricing model has been approved a matter plan will be created. The firm's performance will be tracked against the plan.

The actual fee that will be paid will depend on how well the client feels that the firm has performed. Clients will develop their own scorecards for the firm depending on their own objectives, be it quality of advice, speed of resolution or the law firm's ability to work alongside other firms. Ultimately, considerable discretion remains with the client. Lawyers who have not used value billing previously may not initially feel comfortable with this prospect. However, Crowell & Moring finds that clients are usually more than happy to pay the agreed bonus for a job well done because, having clearly defined objectives in advance, the results tend to speak for themselves.

Once a matter has been completed, key metrics will be stored in an electronic data warehouse. As time goes on, the firm has an increasingly rich source of data points to refer to when setting fees, which ensures that over time the profitability of its AFAs is ever more reliable.

Individual lawyers are provided with financial modeling tools, which they can use to prepare a fee proposal for the matter. They then pass the proposal to a member of Lipstein's team for approval before they are presented to the client. This enables the firm's lawyers to embark on fee negotiations with their clients with a strong hand, knowing that their fee proposals are realistic and are supported by the firm's leadership. Some lawyers are better at using the modelling tools than others. The firm employs business managers in each practice group and fee earners can turn to them for help in creating financial models. This is a good example of support services working with fee earners to buttress the goals of better budgeting, as discussed in Chapter 12.

Value billing in action

Lipstein has provided an example of how value billing might operate in practice from his own case history. One of his specialties is anti-dumping and in this instance an existing client was contemplating instructing Crowell & Moring on an anti-dumping matter for the first time. Anti-dumping legislation exists to protect an economy against the import of goods from another country at a price which is less than their cost of production. In the US, a company which feels that it is being injured by imported goods being sold at less than 'fair value' can apply to the government for an order to be granted imposing duties on goods imported from the dumper's country.

The case in point revolved around an anti-dumping order made in favour of the client, which was coming up for sunset review. From the client's perspective, if the anti-dumping order was not renewed then the value of Crowell & Moring's legal advice would have been low. Whereas if the order was renewed then there would be tremendous value for the business and the client was willing to share the upside with Crowell & Moring. The firm and client agreed a budget for the matter. They then agreed that the client would pay 50 per cent of the budgeted amount as the time costs were incurred. After the first 50 per cent had been paid, the balance of the budget would be earned on a 'double or nothing' basis. In practice, if the order was revoked, then Crowell & Moring would only be entitled to 50 per cent of the agreed budget. On the other hand, if the order was renewed, Crowell & Moring would earn one and a half times the budget amount. In the event, the order was renewed and the client was "more than happy to compensate the firm because the firm had delivered the value that the client was looking for," according to Lipstein.

Impact on the firm

Lipstein notes that hourly billing creates a dissonance between law firms and their clients, who, in an effort to reign in the excessive fees of their law firms, start to issue onerous guidelines and police their firms rigidly. These efforts may be counterproductive and may compel clients to ban firms from holding internal strategy meetings as a result of their fear of being taken advantage of or double charged. By contrast, when working with AFAs, the client and the firm are on the same side of the table and the firm can run the matter in the manner most likely to achieve the best outcome for the client.

Lipstein points out that firms which operate AFAs skilfully may achieve higher profits than those relying on hourly billing. This is particularly the case where a bonus element is included in the AFA. He notes that it's not just about the fee which can be charged. The scorecard process used by clients working on a value-billing basis means that the firm receives a wealth of qualitative commentary on its performance, which it can use to refine its service offering. It also serves to strengthen the relationships between the law firm and its clients.

Value fees, in particular, are more complicated than hourly rates for the firm's financial planners. As fees are dependent on certain events occurring which are not entirely within the control of the firm, there may be a certain 'lumpiness' in cash flow that the firm must be prepared for – and firm and departmental budgets are harder to prepare.

Nonetheless, Crowell & Moring has no doubt that its deployment of AFAs has won clients and new business for the firm and has enhanced profitability. It sees its approach to fees as a means of differentiating the firm in the market place.

The firm's ability to structure profitable fee arrangements which meet clients' needs has helped it to navigate through the recent, volatile economic times.

Client reaction to Crowell & Moring's fee propositions

Not all clients are ready to embrace AFAs. They tend to involve a greater investment of effort before the matter commences and some clients do not have the time or inclination to engage in such discussions. Just as strong firm leadership played a significant role in Crowell & Moring's adoption of AFAs, so too clients who are willing to try AFAs and who receive the most benefit from them tend to be led by strong general counsel, with clear vision for the return on investment to be provided by the legal function.

Lipstein notes that it requires patience to bring some clients round to the idea but once they have tried AFAs they tend to come back for more. Clients who understand AFAs will recognise that they may not reduce their overall spend. Indeed, some pay handsome uplifts to their firms, but they do so willingly because they have played a part in determining the appropriate fee level and their goals have been met.

Continuous improvement and challenges for the future

Currently, approximately 25 to 30 per cent of matters undertaken by Crowell & Moring are performed on the basis of an AFA and the firm urges its clients to make use of the AFAs available.

Although Lipstein expects a hybrid model of AFAs and hourly rates to persist for some time, his goal is for partners at the firm to raise AFAs proactively at the start of every matter, whether speaking to new or to existing clients.

Case study 3: A client perspective

A legal procurement manager discusses procurement objectives and methods, and how law firms can help themselves in negotiations

Procurement objectives

"We are here primarily to save money." So begins an interview with a legal procurement manager (LPM) working for a high-profile UK company. So far, so predictable, but they hasten to qualify this remark by explaining, "That's not something that I would necessarily wholly agree with in the context of buying legal services, which is why I've got the support of the in-house legal team."

The LPM acknowledges that procurement's apparent obsession with saving money can be its downfall in certain areas of the business, such as when buying professional services. "From procurement's point of view, I have to bank the savings but if you just talk about slashing costs, you'll get nowhere with certain stakeholders," he says. The LPM knows that if he approached the general counsel and boldly stated that they were spending too much money on lawyers and needed to cut back, he would be rebuffed. The general counsel would ignore him, complaining, 'You don't understand. It's about quality'. This LPM prefers to characterise his responsibilities as "to get the right firm, of the right quality and at the right cost for the job". His starting point therefore is to find out what the company is outsourcing, why and how. If these questions have not been answered at the outset, then he will be unable to create a review process that will achieve the company's aims.

How procurement teams achieve cost savings

The LPM estimates that since the most recent panel review he orchestrated (alongside the general counsel), the company's legal spend has reduced by 35 per cent. It is clearly worth examining how procurement teams achieve such cost savings for their employers.

Formal processes

Clients often find that just by virtue of undertaking re-tendering exercises, they are able to achieve improved fee rates and additional value-added services from their law firms. Formal processes tend to heighten the competitive tension between incumbent firms. Formal processes can of course be used without the involvement of procurement professionals, but they are a hallmark of procurement-led selection.

In the case of EU public procurement processes or formal auctions, law firms are put under intense pressure to offer the lowest fee rates possible as they may not get a second chance to negotiate if their opening gambits are too high (depending on the type of process followed). Procurement professionals are often more experienced fee negotiators than the lawyers that they work with and possess good, up to date market knowledge to utilise in negotiations. They are therefore more likely to drive down price and increase value-added services than the in-house legal team. They are also unhampered by any existing working relationship with the firms, which may (though not always) hinder a client's negotiating position.

Rigorous contracts

The procurement professional does not simply look at the headline fee rate. If dealing with a procurement professional, law firms are more likely to be forced to enter tight contracts governing the entire relationship. As the LPM admits, these are sometimes "wholly client friendly", but in the current economic conditions, "the hunger is there". Winning a tender may involve law firms investing heavily in staffing dedicated teams but without obtaining any guaranteed minimum spend. Contracts may be notionally for several years to encourage law firms to bid competitively and to invest in relationships. But they may be terminable on short notice. Clients may also reserve the right to go off panel. A particular feature of procurement led contracts is the inclusion of key performance indicators. Examples are:

- Adherence to budgets and deadlines;
- Speed of response; and
- Quality metrics.

All of these are backed up by service credits for poor performance. These tend to be anathema to law firms, which are used to relying on the prestige of their qualifications, the reputations of their firms and their insurance policies. Contracts are also used to assign responsibilities between the client and the law firm. As this LPM says, he uses the process to shift the burden of responsibility for providing an accurate scope of work from the client to the law firm. He notes that traditionally his company has not been good at accurately scoping work, leading to scope creep and fees hugely exceeding budget. Now, his contracts oblige the company's law firms to document any scope creep as it happens and obtain approval. If they do not do this, they will not get paid. "We recognised our weaknesses and 'transferred' them to the law firms," he explains. As a result of incentivising the law firms to manage the client better, he adds that "this has transformed many things about the way we work internally".

Capturing creativity

A common complaint of the private practice lawyer is that when clients ask for creative approaches or innovation, this is simply code for price cuts. This LPM disagrees. He says that he wants to know how law firms can help his company to be more successful and to be better clients. This will ultimately, have the added advantage of reducing fees. He wants to learn what the firms do for other clients to see if the same techniques can be applied at his company. He explains that firms score most highly in the tendering process when they link their value-added services to innovation and continuous improvement. This can go to the heart of whether the firm is providing value and is a legitimate factor to be considered when evaluating a law firm's offering.

Preferred fee structures

The LPM describes this as a case of "horses for courses". Over the years, he has engaged law firms on a variety of different bases. For regular, repeat or fairly standard work types, he has seen huge benefits from adopting fixed fees. However, he also recognises that being able to work with AFAs can require a degree of sophistication from the client, which is not always there. For large scale projects, he has opted for the cheapest hourly rates that he can obtain, rather than AFAs. Currently, he says, his company simply does not possess the necessary data to make informed decisions on AFAs. All this should change. Under his recently established contracts with law firms he will have access to plentiful management information so his aspiration will be to move increasingly to an AFA model – when appropriate for the work type.

How law firms can prepare for negotiations

It is worth noting here that there is a crucial difference between public procurement exercises (at least within the EU) and private procurement exercises. In the latter, clients and law firms are free to run the law firm selection process in whichever manner they choose. There is no need to advertise widely for applicants, parties can reserve the right to make-up and change the rules of the game as they go along. Some face-to-face negotiation meetings are likely to take place and these may incorporate some haggling over price. Under EU public procurement rules by contrast, there is little or no bartering on price (depending on the process followed). Firms tend to have a once and for all shot at submitting a winning fee. Once the official bid has been lodged there is little scope for amendment – the emphasis is on 'clarification' rather than 'negotiation'. The importance of preparation is therefore even more significant than in private procurement exercises.

Know your client

Wise bidders will ask questions prior to submitting their bid. If it is a public procurement exercise, such questions will be answered publicly but anonymously. The LPM counsels bidders to think carefully about the questions that they ask. In trying to establish what the client really wants, a question might give away the firm's competitive advantage and in those circumstances the firm might be wiser to trust its judgement and not to ask the question.

In private processes, bidders are under no such constraints and can ask frank questions about what they are looking for. Often, bidders will have provided legal services to the company before. Those which have done so are immediately at an advantage because of their superior knowledge of the company.

Whether bidding under public or private procurement rules, law firms which have supplied secondees to the company should be particularly well positioned, if the secondees have taken full advantage of the opportunity presented to them by working in-house. As the LPM states, "they are here to do a job but the astute ones will also be here to gather information." He observes that firms which do well in bids or negotiations are those where the secondees have clearly fed back relevant information to their firms. "You see it all over their bids, which is highly intelligent," he says. Not all law firms will be in this fortunate position. In preparing to bid or to enter negotiations, the LPM advises that they should be asking themselves questions such as:

- What is important to the client?
- Where is the client's business going?
- What sort of work and work flow is to be expected?
- What is the client like to deal with?

Know your numbers

Whether entering a face-to-face negotiation or submitting a written bid, it is essential that the fees quoted are supported by a solid analysis of the costs to the firm of conducting the work (as described in

Chapter 5). The procurement professional will want to push the law firm to the lowest point at which work can be performed profitably, but will be concerned that the law firm can still make a profit. It is pointless to put a law firm out of business or to have a firm exit the contract after a few months because it is not proving financially viable. In some procurement situations, price is the most important deciding factor in law firm selection. In others, quality will be more important – or even paramount.

Where price has been emphasised, a firm will not win a tender or a place on the panel unless it can compete on price and show that its pricing has been properly thought through, that it is supported by the firm's business model and that quality of service will not suffer as a result of any compromises the firm may be required to make on price.

The client will also want (contractual) assurances that, where a partner is required to perform the work then a partner will be used – despite the low rates quoted by the firm. Clients do not want to find that low rates lead to work being pushed down to fee earners who are too inexperienced for the matter. This will be backed up by clear contractual requirements that the fee earners named on a job will be used on that job. In some cases, procurement teams may ask to see a breakdown of the firm's costings in order to check that the numbers really do add up. This may particularly be the case where an incumbent supplier offers significant fee reductions when faced with a competitive tender situation, or where premium London firms purport to compete on price with regional firms. The procurement team may ask the firms to explain how they will be able to achieve the pricing that they have offered without compromising quality.

Behaviour to avoid

The bid documentation

When conducting panel reviews, procurement and legal teams tasked with selecting law firms will be presented with reams of paper. Endless pages of black and white text, unrelieved by any graphics, are not very easy for the client to read and can lack impact. Lawyers, the LPM says, are also not best placed to write the bid documents. "You can spot a mile away where the partners have written the bids," he says, Their text tends to be better suited to the legal arena than what is, in effect, a sales document, and they may not bring out the unique selling features that the firm needs to present to the client.

The interview and negotiation

Classic mistakes that law firms make when they get to present their case in person are complacency and lack of preparation. It is a selection interview and, tempting as it may be for an incumbent supplier to argue that they are indispensable to the client, this is not the route to take. The LPM notes that "a bit of humility would go a long way". Complacency can also lead to a lack of preparation. This can manifest itself in bid teams not appearing cohesive, contradicting or talking over each other and not presenting a united front. The LPM notes that these faults are most commonly seen in some of the premier London firms, which expect their reputation for quality to speak for itself. Such firms may be less used to having to bid formally for work and find themselves unable to convey their competitive edge. By contrast, he comments, "the regionals just completely get it because they are perhaps more used to pitching competitively for work". Complacency can also lead firms not to heed client warnings that they will be judged on price. The LPM says that firms that enter initial high bids only to come down significantly in the negotiation lose credibility and force the client to question their seriousness. He cites examples of law firms which reduced their rates by 20 per cent over night when their first bids were rejected. This did not do them any favours. "It makes us suspicious. We'd rather go with the firm which got it right first time," he says.

How to impress

The bid documentation

The LPM strongly urges firms that have sufficient resources to employ the services of professional bid writers, who are able to translate the lawyer's knowledge of the law and their client's needs into a language and style that will convey to the client the benefits of instructing that firm.

Proposals should be easy to read and employ colour, headings and simple charts. In the past, law firms have countered that it is just the LPM who wants charts and that lawyers are not interested in such things, but the LPM states that, "Actually, the people who are most impressed by the graphics are the lawyers." The procurement professional will trudge through all the text (not simply the graphics) to allocate accurate scores to each bid but would stress that, in a competitive environment, visually arresting bids are easier to evaluate – but not at the expense of content.

The interview and negotiation

The composition of the bid team is vital. The LPM says that the team fielded speaks volumes about the firm. He is not impressed by a firm wheeling out the senior partner if that partner is going to have nothing to do with the day-to-day relationship with the client. The firm needs to bring impressive, experienced partners, who will remain involved with the relationship. These partners (or at least the lead partner) need to combine a proven knowledge and understanding of the specialist areas under consideration, with well-developed interpersonal skills. Occasionally, firms can involve more junior personnel to good effect, where those juniors are going to play significant roles in the relationship.

Sometimes, law firms choose to bring their finance director to the bid. This can be very effective where price is a key issue. The role of the finance director would be to provide assurance to the client that the pricing proposals are well thought through and are sustainable for the law firm. By contrast, the LPM has not been impressed by account managers (business development professionals who manage the account) coming to pitches. He has found that they add very little in the context of the negotiation.

In addition to bringing the right people to the negotiation, law firms must explain each person's role both within the law firm and at the meeting. No one should appear redundant. The LPM has spotted a trend for law firms to bring what he calls "dinner mats" – these are letter sized pieces of card or paper, perhaps laminated, which set out photographs of the bid team, their names, roles and the key highlights of their bid. This works best when the bid team sits at the meeting table in the same order that they appear on the dinner mat, thus enabling the client to grasp who is who right from the start, and to recall each person and their contribution after the event.

Finally, each team member should have a clear role in the negotiation and the team should have rehearsed who will lead each part of the meeting. Well-rehearsed teams follow their leader, do not interrupt or contradict each other and appear relaxed and confident. They are "a joy to watch".

PART THREE

Appendices

Appendix 1: Matter plan template

This blank matter plan template has been prepared for illustration purposes only. Templates should always be customised to suit firm and matter requirements. This template is for a corporate lawyer acting on a purchase of a company by means of the acquisition of 100 per cent of the share capital of the company. Seller and purchaser are both UK private limited companies and the law firm is acting for the purchaser.

Task	Details	Chargeable hours by fee earner type				Sub total
		Partner	Snr asst	Jnr asst	Trainee	
	Initiating discussions and establishing relationships					
1.	Take instructions, compose and brief team					
2.	Confidentiality agreement					
3.	Engagement letters of accountants, bankers and other professional advisers					
4.	Hold harmless letters, if law firm is to use materials produced by other professionals					
5.	Letter of intent (LOI)					
6.	Exclusivity agreement					
	Due diligence					
7.	Attendance at data room/review of due diligence materials online					
8.	Processing supplementary Q&A					
9.	Further research – for example, pensions risk, litigation risk, environmental contamination					
10.	Attendance at management presentations and acting on information					
11.	Production of report					
	Structuring					
12.	Tax advice					
13.	Setting up acquisition vehicle					
	Sale documentation					
14.	Sale and purchase agreement and warranty schedule					
15.	Disclosure letter					
16.	Completion accounts schedule					
17.	Ancillary documentation – for example, pension schedule, tax covenant, property schedule, as applicable					
18.	Attendance at signing meeting for exchange of contracts					

	Completion					
19.	Escrow Agreement (for example, if there is retention of purchase price)					
20.	Transitional services agreement/software licences					
21.	Checking satisfaction of conditions precedent (may include regulatory clearances, see below)					
22.	Preparation for and attendance at completion meeting					
	Anti-trust and regulatory advice and clearances					
23.	Summary information goes here. Details would be set out in a separate matter template					
	Funding arrangements					
24.	Summary information goes here. Details would be set out in a separate matter template					
	Post-completion matters					
	Most of this will be handled by the buyer directly but typical legal work includes:					
25.	Registration of charges					
26.	Release of escrow					
27.	Compilation of deal bible					
	Other post-completion issues, such as integration projects and redundancy programmes may be billed separately as new matters					
	Co-ordination					
28.	Team briefings					
29.	Client briefings					
	Totals					

Appendix 2: Matter budget template

This blank matter budget template has been prepared for illustration purposes only. Templates should always be customised to suit firm and matter requirements.

Hourly statistics					
	Partner	Snr asst	Jnr asst	Trainee	
Standard rate					
Recovered rate					
Hourly salary cost					
Margin					

Matter plan					
	Chargeable hours by fee earner type				
Details	Partner	Snr asst	Jnr asst	Trainee	Sub total
Totals					

Matter total fees					
	Partner	Snr asst	Jnr asst	Trainee	Total
Standard fees					
Recovered fees					
Salary cost					

Matter margins				
	Standard	Recovered	Variance	
Fees				
Salary cost				
Gross margin				
Gross margin %				
Operating profit				
Operating profit margin %				

Adapted from materials provided by Robert Mowbray of Taylor Mowbray LLP, with thanks.

Appendix 3: Pre-negotiation checklist

Engagement status		
		Firm's leverage
Competitive tender for new client	☐	Low
Competitive tender for new business from existing client	☐	Mid
Instructed subject to agreement on price	☐	High
Matter underway	☐	Mid
Matter completed	☐	Low

Client factors
These factors will impact client's attitude to fees, cost to the firm and willingness to discount

Priorities	Result	Right answer	Speed	Cost	Value	Named lawyer
	☐	☐	☐	☐	☐	☐
Matter importance	High	Mid	Low			
	☐	☐	☐			
Style	Helpful	Demanding	Detailed	High level	Pragmatic	Bureaucratic
	☐	☐	☐	☐	☐	☐
Status	Major client of firm	Major client of practice area	Growth potential	New	One-off	
	☐	☐	☐	☐	☐	

Matter budget	
Expected matter cost to firm	
Target profit margin for this client matter	
Target fee	
BATNA	
Walk away	

Easy trades			
Increase fee		**Reduce fee**	
Value-added services	☐	Regular payment schedule	☐
Speed	☐	Agreed retainer	☐
Risk share	☐	Guaranteed future instruction/exclusivity	☐

Value proposition	
Increase client's financial returns	☐
Improve client's processes/systems	☐
Reduce client's risk	☐
Technical ability	☐
Track record in this field or sector or geography	☐
Global reach	☐
Resources	☐
Contacts	☐
Knowledge of client	☐
Creative fee structures	☐
Risk share	☐
Price guarantee	☐
Payment terms/finance options	☐
Value-added services	☐
Speed	☐
Satisfaction guarantee	☐
Other	☐

Pricing proposals			
	Structure*	**Fee range**	**Margin****
Option 1			
Option 2			
Option 3			

* *Hourly/fixed/capped/collars/success/holdbacks/credits/value/retainer/other*
** *Alternative options should change structure or re-engineer work to maintain margin*

Index

www.ingramcontent.com/pod-product-compliance
Ingram Content Group UK Ltd.
Pitfield, Milton Keynes, MK11 3LW, UK
UKHW050231160926
8657IPUK00008B/191

9 781907 787935